To: J

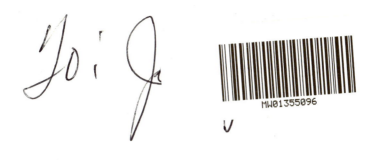

Only a Look

A Historical Look at the Career of Mrs. Roberta Martin and the
Roberta Martin Gospel Singers of Chicago, Illinois

Ronald L. Greer

Copyright © 2015 Ronald L. Greer.

All rights reserved. No part of this book may be used or reproduced by any means, graphic, electronic, or mechanical, including photocopying, recording, taping or by any information storage retrieval system without the written permission of the author except in the case of brief quotations embodied in critical articles and reviews.

This book is a work of non-fiction. Unless otherwise noted, the author and the publisher make no explicit guarantees as to the accuracy of the information contained in this book and in some cases, names of people and places have been altered to protect their privacy.

WestBow Press books may be ordered through booksellers or by contacting:

WestBow Press
A Division of Thomas Nelson & Zondervan
1663 Liberty Drive
Bloomington, IN 47403
www.westbowpress.com
1 (866) 928-1240

Because of the dynamic nature of the Internet, any web addresses or links contained in this book may have changed since publication and may no longer be valid. The views expressed in this work are solely those of the author and do not necessarily reflect the views of the publisher, and the publisher hereby disclaims any responsibility for them.

Any people depicted in stock imagery provided by Thinkstock are models, and such images are being used for illustrative purposes only.
Certain stock imagery © Thinkstock.

ISBN: 978-1-5127-0897-4 (sc)
ISBN: 978-1-5127-0898-1 (e)

Library of Congress Control Number: 2015913584

Print information available on the last page.

WestBow Press rev. date: 9/17/2015

I feel so honored to be part of and just a minor part of a book being written about my mother and the group that she loved so dearly: The Roberta Martin Singers.

I read an article written two days after her Passing and it said, ***"A Legacy Passed This Way"***. I was very blessed and privileged to be the only person who got to see her on a daily basis: as her only child. Although many pondered and speculated about the lady that they called, "Mrs. Martin"; I witnessed firsthand her many talents, her quiet nature, her laughter, her sadness and her love of everyone she met. And in all my years of knowing my mother; she never, ever displayed an angry moment.

I am eternally grateful to have Ronald devote an enormous amount of time and document the short, but well spent life of my mother and the singers that she adored.

I am happy to endorse this book and dedicate it to the memory of my mother: Mrs. Roberta Martin Austin and her devoted singers-The Roberta Martin Singers of Chicago, Illinois.

Truly a legacy passed this way and I thank God that I had the opportunity to be part of her life.

Leonard J. "Sonny" Austin
Son of Jimmy and Roberta Martin Austin

Mrs. Roberta Evelyn Winston Martin Austin

LITERARY DEDICATION:

First, I am pleased to dedicate this book posthumously to the memory of my mother: ***Mrs. Elizabeth Ellen Monroe Greer:*** a woman whose countless and uncanny support gave me the determination I needed to continue the endless hours of research in order to complete this historical book.

Next, I want to dedicate this book to the son of the late Roberta Martin and Jimmy Austin: ***Mr. Leonard Austin of Miami, Florida.*** A born again, college educated gentleman of stature: who graciously gave me his blessing and shared with me his most intimate photo collection in order to enhance this book about his mother, her singers and their many historical accomplishments.

Most Importantly, I would like to dedicate this book to the families of those members touched by the life and legacy of Roberta Evelyn Winston Martin Austin:

To the descendants of the brothers and sisters of Roberta Martin

- James Hamilton
- William Hamilton
- Beatrice Winston Hall
- LeGessa Winston Brown
- Fontaine Winston
- Fred Winston

To the descendants of the late Mrs. Leona Price - Mrs. Martin's Secretary & Business Manager of the Martin Studio of Gospel Music

To the remaining living members of the Roberta Martin Sangers:

>Romance Watson
>Stanley Harold Johnson
>Louise McCord Williams

And to the memory of and families of those members of the Roberta Martin Singers who have left this life and are singing with Mrs. Martin in heaven:

>Eugene Smith
>Norsalus McKissick
>Willie Webb
>Robert Anderson
>James Lawrence
>Bessie Folk
>Little Lucy Smith
>Sadie Durrah-Nolan
>Ardie B. Smith Phillips
>Myrtle Scott
>Myrtle Jackson
>Gloria Griffin
>Archie Dennis, Jr.
>Delois Barrett Campbell

SPECIAL ACKNOWLEDGEMENT

A very special posthumous acknowledgement goes to the person who taught me and "schooled" me on just about everything that I know about Mrs. Roberta Martin Austin and The Roberta Martin Singers: from their pioneering beginnings in 1933 to their latter day reign as premier ambassadors of gospel music. For 33 years, from 1976 until his passing in 2009; Eugene and I conversed continually on a daily basis: talking about the life and career of the Martin Singers including many of the groups funniest moments and most serious situations.

This very special acknowledgement goes to, who, for many years served as the Business Manager of the group: the late Mr. Eugene Thomas Smith (1921-2009)

Eugene Thomas Smith
Photo: courtesy of Bob Marovich of Chicago, Illinois

SPECIAL POSTHUMOUS THANKS TO...

The late Mr. James Austin – who introduced me to Eugene Smith in 1976 at a time when I was researching and searching for historical knowledge about the Roberta Martin Singers.

During the course of time that I began conversing with Eugene in 1976; he introduced me to several of the Martin Singers of which I owe a gratitude of thankfulness for their knowledge and historical information:

Ms. Bessie Folk – who shared with me her many adventures while singing as a member of the group.

Mrs. Delois Barrett Campbell – who told me many stories of how Mrs. Martin would sing, get "happy" in church and how she would teach her songs

Mr. Robert Anderson – who shared with me how he filled in for Mrs. Martin at the Chicago Baptist Convention in the early 1940's and how she and Eugene were instrumental in his developing of the Good Shephard Singers.

He also shared as how they (the boys back in the days) would cut up back when they were kids and all Mrs. Martin would have to do is give them the "look".

Rev. Archie Dennis, Jr. – who shared with me his memories of traveling on the train with the Martin Singers and how the concept of the song "When He Calls My Name" was conceived.

Mrs. Lucy Smith "Little Lucy" Collier – who shared with me so much information about the group; about the musical construction and even information about her famous grandmother: Elder Lucy Smith and most importantly- how she played matchmaker for her father and Mrs. Martin.

Although not enough can be stated as to how Eugene helped me with this book; through the combined efforts of he and the aforementioned singers; my well of knowledge about this pioneering institution "ranneth over".

SPECIAL THANKS TO ...

Bob Marovich - Chicago, Illinois - famed gospel music historian, internet blogger, author of "A City Called Heaven" and radio host of "Gospel Memories" over WLUW. Bob has been both a personal and professional inspiration to me in the completion of this book. He also serves as my literary mentor.

Joseph Middleton - Houston, Texas - *creator* of the "Golden Era Gospel Blog". His insight and various social media connections and information helped to enhance the already stored knowledge that I attained from Eugene Smith concerning the history of the Roberta Martin Singers.

Dr. Stanley Keeble - Chicago, Illinois - the owner and CEO of the Gospel Heritage Museum; musical protégé of Willie Webb; and close friend of Mrs. Roberta Martin and the members of the Martin Singers. His knowledge and insight of their working together was a true treasure of untold knowledge.

Kenji Bolden – Emporia, Kansas – the only person alive: that I am aware of; whose piano playing style is truly duplicative of that of Roberta Martin and Little Lucy Smith. He has devoted his post secondary education career to further studying the musical style of Roberta Martin and has incorporated that into his everyday musical studies: both on a personal and professional level.

Jordan Phillips – Gaffney, South Carolina – a very special thanks for creating the front and back cover design for the book and for your superb marketing skills.

Photographer Disclaimer

Unless specifically indicated; the following pictures housed within this book are (were) from the collection of the late Eugene Smith. It was Eugene Smith who gave me consent to use any and all of these pictures in the creation of this book. Several pictures within the book were from the collection of the late Mrs. Lucy Smith Collier: stepdaughter of Roberta Martin of which were donated to the Chicago Public Library and are housed in the Vivian Harsh Research collection of Afro-American History and Literature. These photos are labeled accordingly. Many of the pictures in this book are also from the private collection of Leonard "Sonny" Austin. Also, special thanks to Rev. Stanley Keeble of the Gospel Heritage Museum and Rev. Issac Whitmon for supplying a priceless photo.

INTRODUCTION

As the old saying goes, "every now and then", there comes along a person that exhibits strong Christian ethics, grace and charm. One such person was the legendary woman of gospel music: **Mrs. Roberta Martin.** A woman who, in later years, was destined to shake the music world and the gospel music world in particular with one of the greatest gospel singing groups of all time which contained a virtual Who's Who stable of gospel singers that ever existed in the cultural genre of African-American music: **The Roberta Martin Singers of Chicago.**

LET'S TAKE A JOURNEY BACK THROUGH TIME . . . . .

In the 1920's; **Thomas Andrew Dorsey,** an accomplished blues musician from Villa Rica, Georgia was creating and developing a new standard in blues music. He, along with legendary blues performer **Gertrude "Ma" Rainey** were swiftly becoming a household name within the realm of African-American music with their famous blues selections. His compositions for the great "Ma" Rainey were considered classics and legendary: even back in the 1920's. As Thomas Dorsey said in the movie, "Say Amen, Somebody"; *"God told me I needed to change my ways"* and Blues genius Thomas Dorsey received salvation and left the world of blues music. His barrelhouse piano style of playing would carry over into the formation of a new music in the 1920's called **"Gospel".**

Although an early "gospel style" form of music had a foothold in most of the Holiness and/or "Sanctified" churches in the southern regions of the United States prior to its formal existence in the 1920's; this style of music was formally adopted in the worship setting by the National Baptist Convention in 1921.

Many scattering seeds of gospel music had been planted in Chicago's gospel community even before Dorsey's entrance.

William Roberts (1876-1954), a Mississippian who was saved under the ministry of Bishop Charles Harrison Mason, moved to Chicago in 1917 to plant a church. Under the pastorate of Pastor Wm. Roberts, gospel music was introduced to the small South Side congregation.

Another southerner, **Charles Henry Pace (1886-1963)** moved to Chicago from Atlanta Georgia and came under the influence of gospel music. He later incorporated the music at Chicago's Liberty Baptist Church.

These two men were major influences that laid the groundwork for gospel music to have its founding roots in Chicago when Dorsey sprang on the scene. Nevertheless, the team of Thomas Dorsey, Theodore Frye and his singing sensation Sallie Martin would be credited as the founders of the "new" gospel sound: a sound deriving from a mixture of the Blues from the old South, the sophisticated sound of Scott Joplin's Ragtime and the smooth uptown classy sound of Jazz. All of these forms of music were popular during the early piano days of Thomas A. "Georgia Tom" Dorsey. These three forms of music helped to mold the piano playing style of Thomas Dorsey: of which he used in the creative mixture of the new gospel sounding genre.

After his conversion to Christianity; it was ironic that one of the most famous hymns would be composed by Dorsey. This happened after he encountered a personal tragedy that would change his life forever. This is what happened:

> *Dorsey was summoned to St. Louis to assist in the organizing of a gospel choir. While enroute there, his wife Nettie Harper Dorsey, who was in the last stages of her pregnancy, died due to complications in childbirth. The baby: Thomas Andrew Dorsey, Jr., was born without difficulty. But after a few days, the newborn baby died. Grieving and distressed, Dorsey didn't know what to do. After a few days of solitude, Prof. Dorsey confided in his friend, Theodore Roosevelt Frye for strength. When Dorsey would pray to the Lord for strength, Frye replied, "don't just say Lord, say Precious Lord". That phrase stuck with Dorsey and not many days afterwards, he composed the most famous song in the history of gospel music: "Precious Lord-Take My Hand".*

When Thomas Dorsey, Frye: and the assistance of his soloist Sallie Martin formed this new sound, it was criticized heavily by the African American clergy of that day. Many preachers called the music blasphemy against the Lord and several singers were kept out of churches. But none of that stopped Dorsey as he was on a course set forth by God himself.

This new style of music called "**Gospel**" was created heavily by using Dorsey's piano playing methods that had been inspired by his song versions from his days of playing and traveling with "Ma" Rainey. This "barrelhouse" style was carried over into the early versions of several gospel tunes written and arranged by Dorsey. "If You See My Savior" unmistakably carries the same tune as Ma Rainey's "Touch No Man".

Like the blues, early gospel music was known for it's profound religious lyrics and the barrelhouse style of the piano laying down the musical accompaniment. With strong spiritual determination, by the time the 1930's rolled around, Thomas Dorsey and Sallie Martin had set gospel music on a path of tolerable acceptance within the church setting.

But in the midst of the Thomas Dorsey/Sallie Martin reign of Gospel Music in Chicago, a God-fearing woman was shaping into an accomplished pianist, arranger, composer, directress and singer. This woman, in later years, would become one of the main focal points in the field of gospel music and one of the greatest pioneers in the field of African-American music. Born in Helena, Arkansas and moving to Chicago at an early age, she would soon meet music master, Dr. Theodore Roosevelt Frye: a man who would become the inspiration of her life and enhance her musical skills greatly. Therefore, in due season, **Roberta Evelyn Winston** would soon become a pivotal part of the Black American culture with the formation of one of the greatest gospel groups ever: **The Roberta Martin Singers of Chicago, Illinois.**

Martin & Frye Quartet (1933-1936)
Roberta Martin Singers (1936-1969)

Roberta Evelyn Winston Martin Austin - (1933-1969)
Eugene Smith - (1934-1969)
Norsalus McKissick- (1933-1969)
Willie Webb (1933-1949; 53-56)
Robert Anderson - (1933-1939)
James Lawrence - (1933 - 1940's)
* W.C. Herman - (1933 -?)
Lost his life in World War 2

* Ardie B. Smith Phillips (1935-1936)
According to a conversation with the late Eugene Smith,
He stated that Mrs. Phillips was truly the
first female- singer of the group.
She was known as the "Anthem Soloist" for the early Martin-Frye Quartet during a time when the Roberta Martin and her singers repertoire relied heavily on hymns and anthems.

- Phyllis Hall: writer of He Knows How Much We Can Bear briefly sang The Roberta Martin Singers in late 1940 - 1941

Bessie Folk - (1939-1950; 1955; 1962)
Sadie Durrah Nolan - (1945-1947)
Delois Barrett Campbell - (1943-1965; 68-69)
"Little" Lucy Smith Collier - (1949-1952; 57-69)
Romance Watson - (1949-1958)
Myrtle Scott - (1951-52)
Myrtle Jackson - (1951-52)

* During the period from 1949-1957; several singers "freelanced" or sang sporadically with the Roberta Martin Singers including:
Delores Taliferro (known as Della Reese)
Ozella Mosely Clifton & Ann Yancey

Gloria Griffin - (1957-1969)
Archie Dennis - (1958-1959; 62-69)
Harold Johnson - (1959-1962)
Louise McCord - (1966)

The Roberta Martin Singers
A Historical Timeline

1929   Roberta Martin began playing the piano at the Arnett Chapel Methodist Church in Morgan Park

1932   Roberta Martin began playing the piano at the Ebenezer Baptist Church- along with Prof. Theodore R. Frye

1933   The Martin & Frye Quartet was organized at the Ebenezer Baptist Church in Chicago, Illinois

1934   Eugene Smith became a member of the Martin & Frye Quartet

1935   Mrs. Addie B. Smith Phillips sang briefly with the Martin & Frye Quartet

1936   The Martin & Frye Quartet became known as The Roberta Martin Singers

1938   The Roberta Martin Singers travelled with Prof. E. Clifford Davis and his wife, Madame Mary Johnson Davis throughout the Northeastern USA

         The Martin Studio of Gospel Music was established.

1939   The Roberta Martin Singers briefly became known as the "Martin & Martin Singers: with the association of Sallie Martin. Bessie Folk became the first female singer in the all male group.

1943   Delois Barrett Campbell became the second female singer in the group

1945   Mrs. Sadie Durrah-Nolan became a member of the group.
According to Eugene Smith, the Roberta Martin Singers recorded a vanity record in California. Other sources have the record session as 1949.

1947   The Roberta Martin Singers made their first official professional recording or Fidelity Records. Also, Saddie Durrah-Nolan passed away.

1949   The Roberta Martin Singers began recording for Apollo Records. Also, Romance Watson began singing with the group.

1951   Myrtle Scott began singing with the Roberta Martin Singers.

1952   Myrtle Jackson began singing with the Roberta Martin Singers.

1957   The Roberta Martin Singers began recording for Savoy Records. Gloria Griffin began singing with the group.

1958   The Roberta Martin Singers recorded "GRACE" and "GOD SPECIALIZES"

1959   Archie Dennis began singing with the Roberta Martin Singers

1960   The Roberta Martin Singers received two gold records from the Apollo Recording Company for Only A Look and The Old Ship of Zion.

         Mrs. Roberta Martin Austin directed the 1000 voice choir of the National Baptist Convention.

         Harold Johnson began singing with the Roberta Martin Singers

1961   Archie Dennis returned home from active military service.

1963   The Roberta Martin Singers recorded their first and only "live" recording, entitled, "From Out Of Nowhere".
         The Roberta Martin Singers traveled to Spoleto, Italy to sing at the Music Festival of Two Worlds.

	Professor Theodore Roosevelt Frye, the man who mentored Roberta Martin passed away.
1965	Roberta Martin wrote and directed a play called "What God Hath Wrought" about the evolution of Gospel Music.
1969	Mrs. Roberta Martin Austin passed away.
1979	Mrs. Leona Price, Business Manager for the Martin Studio of Gospel Music retired after over 40 years of service.
1981	The Roberta Martin Singers were honored at the Smithsonian Institute in Washington, D.C., for their musical contribution.,
1982	Mr. James "Jimmy" Austin: the husband of Mrs. Roberta Martin and the father of "Little" Lucy Smith Collier passed away
1990	James Lawrence, an original member of the Martin & Frye Quartet passed away.
1994	Members of the Roberta Martin Singers sang at a Black Gospel legends reunion: sponsored by Bill and Gloria Gather

1995   Gloria Griffin, Myrtle Scott and Robert Anderson: all former Members of the Martin Singers passed away.

1997   Norsalus McKissick passed away in Philadelphia.

1998   The United States Postal Service issued a postage stamp honoring Mrs. Roberta Martin

1999   Professor Willie J. Webb passed away

2001   Bessie Folk and Rev. Archie Dennis, Jr., passed away

2009   Eugene Smith, the Business Manager of the Roberta Martin Singers passed away.

2010   "Little" Lucy Smith Collier: the step daughter of Mrs. Roberta Martin and founder of the Lucy Smith Singers passed away.

2011   Mrs. Delois Barrett Campbell passed away.

The Roberta Martin Studio of Gospel Music Chicago, Illinois

Here are some of the various publications and sheet music from the Martin Studio of Gospel Music: from its inception through the 1960's`
all documents published by permission from Leonard Austin

various early songbooks published in the 1940's by the Martin Studio of Gospel Music

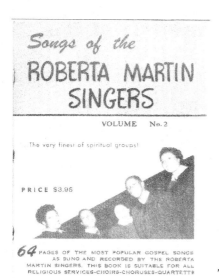 This songbook came in four (4) different volumes and featured songs recorded by the group primarily on Apollo Records

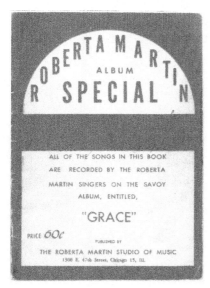 This songbook was one of their best sellers. It featured sheet music from two of their best sellers: GRACE and GOD SPECIALIZES

the Two Theme Songs of The Roberta Martin Singers

"Is Your All On The Altar" was the theme song of the "Martin and Frye Quartet and the Roberta Martin Singers: prior to 1943.

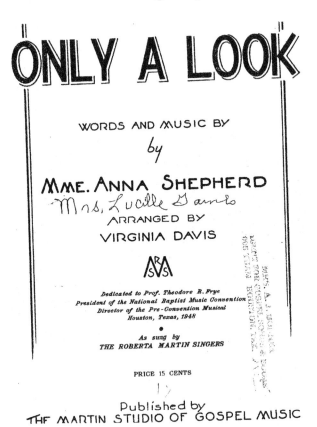

In mid 1940's; **"Only A Look"** *became the theme song of the Roberta Martin Singers. Because of its spiritual message, the group recorded it twice: originally on Apollo Records with Bessie Folk as lead and on Savoy Records with Delois Barrett Campbell as lead vocalist.*

Mrs. Martin enjoying a "mother-son moment" surrounded by sheet music.

Mrs. Martin surrounded by her love for children. Sonny is in the cowboy hat.
Both photos provided by Leonard Austin collection.

The Roberta Martin Singers Gold Records

During the course of their career (1933-1969); the Roberta Martin Singers were the recipients of six Gold Records: 2 from Apollo Records and 4 from Savoy Records.

APOLLO RECORDS:

1. **The Old Ship of Zion – led by Norsalus McKissick**
2. **Only A Look – led by Bessie Folk**

SAVOY RECORDS:

3. **Grace – led by Norsalus McKissick**
4. **God Specializes – led by Gloria Griffin**
5. **God Is Still On The Throne – led by Gloria Griffin**
6. **Try Jesus, He Satisfies – led by Roberta Martin**

Mrs. Roberta Martin receiving a "Gold Record" from Bess Berman of Apollo Records.
(left to right): Norsalus McKissick; Bess Berman- owner Apollo Records; Roberta Martin;
Delois Barrett; Eugene Smith; and unidentified gentleman. "Sonny" Austin is standing in front of Eugene Smith. *Photo: courtesy of Leonard Austin collection*

Mrs. Roberta Martin being presented a Gold Record from Savoy Records executive: Herman Lubinsky for the album, "GRACE". *Photo: courtesy of Leonard Austin*

AWARDED GOLD DISC—Roberta Martin, famed leader of the Martin Singers, was presented a gold record in recognition of the fact the group's records are selling in the hundreds of thousands. The Martin Singers have gained the reputation of being the finest spiritual troupe in the country. Carl Lebow of Apollo Records is making the presentation to Miss Martin, while Charles Lajoie of Hill and Range music publishers, and Miss Martin's son look on.

(from Color Magazine, 1953)
By permission of Leonard Austin

The 1930's

Roberta Evelyn Martin:
The Lady, Her Singers & Her Music
*"The Early years of the Martin & Frye Quartet &
The Roberta Martin Singers"*

As the late gospel historian, Dr. Clayton L. Hannah wrote in his liner notes to the 1979 Savoy album, *"The Best of the Roberta Martin Singers,* " Although Thomas Dorsey is credited as the originator and Mahalia Jackson received the highest acclaim, Roberta Martin without a doubt made the greatest contribution. She created and left a dynasty of unmatched gospel singers and a portfolio of unduplicated gospel music".

Roberta Evelyn Winston, the daughter of William and Anna Winston: proprietors of a local general store; was born in Helena Arkansas (Phillips County) on **February 14, 1907:** according to Census records. *Some accounts have her birth year as 1912. Her son, Leonard Austin always said that his mother would have been 57 on her birthday, but she passed away the month before. With that statement, Roberta Martin's birthdate would have been in 1912.*

She would grow to be an innate young lady: instilled with deep, sensitive Christian values and beliefs. At the age of 8; she, along with her parents and siblings: *William and James Hamilton, Beatrice, Fred, LeGessa and Fontaine Winston* migrated to Cairo, Illinois and then on to Chicago, Illinois: following in the fashion of many other African American families from the deep South and southern United States- who were escaping the oppression left by the deep rootedness of slavery. It was in the city of Chicago where Roberta completed her formal educational training at the Wendell Phillips High School and post secondary education from Northwestern University.

As a young girl, Roberta would pick tunes on the family piano; but it was not until she had formal piano training from her sister-in-law that her aspirations to become a concert pianist became known.

Her musical talents were "polished" through the tutorage of her music teacher, Dr. Mildred Jones Bryant and other professors from the Music Conservatory of Chicago where Roberta attended as a student. While at both the Northwestern University and the Music Conservatory, Roberta spent much of her time studying such great composers as Bach, Beethoven, Brahms, Strauss and Schubert. However two people: a young man named William Martin and a singer by the name of Bertha Wise would come into her life and change the course of her journey forever.

In the late 1920's as a young lady, Roberta Winston would meet and marry a gentleman by the name of **William "Bill" Martin**. Eventhough that union would be short lived and the details of their subsequent divorce were unknown- Roberta would receive something very valuable from that union: *a last name change* - which would soon become renowned within the circles of African-American Christian (Protestant) churches. Therefore, in marriage; Miss Roberta Winston became ***Mrs. Roberta Martin.***

Bert, as she was called, really became interested in gospel music after she heard an early day gospel or "Jubilee" singer **Bertha Wise and her singers: The Wise Singers from Augusta Georgia.** As they were traveling in the Chicago area, they were singing at the Ebenezer Baptist Church where Roberta Martin heard them sing *"I Can Tell The World About This"*. As Roberta Martin stated in a 1964 interview:

> *I'd been playing in churches nearly all my life. I started down at Ebenezer Baptist Church, where I was the pianist for the Sunday School. At that time, I was just interested in church hymns, anthems, choir music and secular songs. The first time I heard gospel singing as such was this lady and the men - Bertha Wise and her Singers from Augusta Georgia. Miss Wise played the piano for them. They came to our church and oh did we enjoy them.*

Roberta, who was divorced from her then husband, William Martin, acquired her first church position as pianist for the Arnett Chapel Methodist Church in Chicago's Morgan Park suburb in **1929**. While serving as pianist for the church, she was discovered by Prof. Theodore Roosevelt Frye, a leading authority in gospel music and Director of Church Music at the Ebenezer Baptist Church. Roberta's musical talents were so unique that it caught the eye and ear of Prof. Frye. From their first conversation that convened between Roberta Martin and Frye, it seemed that they were destined to become a close musical dynasty.

During this time, Prof. Frye was directing the Ebenezer Bapt. Church choir and Prof. Thomas Dorsey along with Mrs. Mabel Sanford Lewis were serving as musical accompanists. As the story goes, Pilgrim was invited to Ebenezer for a Sunday Fellowship service. When Rev. J.C. Austin, the pastor of Pilgrim heard the gospel chorus, he fell under the spell of the gospel sound. He then later asked Thomas Dorsey to come to Pilgrim and assume the duties of musical director and to organize a Gospel Chorus. When Dorsey agreed to go to Pilgrim, a vacancy would arise at the Piano at the Ebenezer church. Frye, remembering the musical talents of Roberta Martin, contacted her at the Arnett Chapel Methodist Church and asked her if she would like to become the pianist at the Ebenezer Bapt. Church. Without hesitation, Roberta Martin accepted the invitation.

Professor Theodore Roosevelt Frye
the man who discovered and mentored Roberta Martin

In 1932, Roberta Martin became the official pianist for the Ebenezer Baptist Church and the capable Theodore *(Professor)* Frye maintained his duties as Choir Director and Minister of Music. After serving in her capacity for a period of time, she was approached and asked by the pastor, the late Rev. J.H. Lorenzo Smith if she would organize a Jr. Gospel Chorus.

Roberta, being a Christian woman of deep faith, sought the Lord for an answer. When she received her answer, to her announcement, over 300 children came forth. Roberta Martin had made history: organizing one of the first Junior Gospel Choruses in the history of the Black church. Before that time, many of the churches of that day only had singing performed by the entire congregation or if there was a choir, it was either the Senior Choir- comprised mainly of adults or the Jr. Choir- composed of children. Nevertheless, both choirs sang hymns and anthems. Gospel music was truly a musical rarity.

This is where it all began . .

The 1932 Ebenezer Baptist Church Jr. Gospel Chorus - Chicago, Illinois
out of this group came the "original" Martin & Frye Quartet in 1933
front: Mrs. Mable Sanford Lewis – Prof. Theodore R. Frye – Ms. Roberta Martin
photo courtesy: Eugene Smith collection

When Roberta Martin organized the Jr. Gospel Chorus at the Ebenezer Baptist Church, part of her organizational focus was to appoint several Jr. Gospel Chorus members to key leadership positions. First, she recruited a young lad named Willie Webb as pianist, Master James Lawrence served as Director and Ms. Martin stepped out of the limelight and took the reins as General Overseer.

Soon afterwards, the 4th Sunday of each month became known as *"Youth Day at Ebenezer"*. On that Sunday, the Jr. Gospel Chorus: under the leadership of Roberta Martin and the Jr. Choir, under the directorship of Mrs. Mabel Sanford Lewis brought jubilistic music to the throngs of parishioners in Sunday morning worship.

The musical celebration was carried over into the 4th Sunday Night service when the Jr. Gospel Chorus and the Jr. Choir presented their monthly musical. Chicago gospel music talents **H.V. Caruthers, Roberta Martin, Theodore Frye and Willie Webb** came together for that occasion. It soon grew to such a notable affair that many worshipers would venture to the program, many, many hours before the service: just to get a good seat. The jammed packed Ebenezer Baptist Church, which housed the historical event still stands at 4501 S. Vincennes Avenue in Chicago.

1933 brought such joy and excitement to the heart of Dr. Frye as the Jr. Gospel Chorus: under the direction of Ms. Roberta Martin was an instant success: receiving spiritual acceptance from both the pastorate and the parishioners of the Ebenezer Baptist Church. Seeing the success of several solo singers within the chorus: Frye urged Roberta Martin to take special note in the harmonies and talents of four lads within the chorus:

James Lawrence-their director

Willie Webb - their pianist
and two soloist: Norsalus McKissick & Robert Anderson

After hearing the harmonies of these singers, she, along with Prof. Frye created what was to become one of the greatest groups and most influential singing groups in African American musical history: ***The Martin & Frye Quartet.*** This group would become known in later years as ***The Roberta Martin Singers.***

Mrs. Martin and the Martin & Frye Quartet began singing in Chicago and in the surrounding areas at many of the black churches: carrying the gospel in song to the hearts of the people. Soon afterwards, the name of Roberta Martin and the Martin & Frye Gospel Quartet became a popular fixture in many black churches in Chicago's Southside. No matter how musically appealing many other church choirs and choruses were: the masses flocked to 4501 S. Vincennes Ave. to witness the gospel in song under the leadership of Roberta Martin and Theodore Frye. Although the Convention of National Gospel Choirs and Choruses; which began in 1932 with Thomas Dorsey, Theodore Frye, Beatrice Brown, Sallie Martin, Magnolia Lewis Butts and St. Louis' own Willie Mae Ford Smith was designed to promote gospel music within many black protestant churches; the whole talk of the Southside community in Chicago and surrounding areas was of the Ebenezer Jr. Gospel Chorus and the newly formed Martin & Frye Quartet.

While all of these musical extravaganzas were happening on Chicago's Southside of town, another very important figure in gospel music was getting his roots embodied on the other side of Chicago. At the Salem Baptist Church, a young lad by the name of ***Eugene Thomas Smith***; the son of the late Scott and Eugenia Smith was being groomed into an accomplished singer: through the aid of his music teacher, Mrs. Anna Bright.

When the National Baptist Convention came to Chicago, Eugene's pastor: Rev. B.L. Rose, hosted the affair and invited Eugene to sing. Clothed in a white suit with white high top shoes, he sang to thousands. After a stellar performance at the National Baptist Convention, Eugene Smith acquired the title of "The Boy Wonder" Singer. Seeing the potential that Eugene possessed, Mrs. Bright sought to get Eugene exposure in the area churches around Chicago. Through some persistence, Eugene was found singing in the Sunday morning worship service at Ebenezer Baptist Church: in the presence of Ms. Roberta Martin. When Eugene sang the lyrics:

> ***Houses and land I, may not own - But wealth and riches to be known - Little person, in this race, I may be***
> ***I don't keep up, with the times - But I know I'm doing fine***
> ***I claim Jesus first, and that's enough for me . . . . .***

Roberta Martin knew that Gene was a born singer. Not long after the service, Roberta Martin: with the blessings of Professor Frye: sought to ask Eugene's mother, Mrs. Eugenia Smith, if he could become a member of the Martin

& Frye Quartet. Eugene's mother quickly replied joyously to the invitation. That meeting would be the start of a long and deep relationship and partnership between Eugene Smith and Roberta Martin. That was in **1934**.

Eugene recalled to Bob Marovich in an interview how he met Roberta Martin:

Oh yeah, okay, I sang at the National Baptist Convention, and Dr. Smith who was the pastor of the church heard me and invited me to come to Ebenezer and sing in his Sunday morning service. And of course when I got there, I didn't know who was going to play for me, so I asked, they gave me a seat down front there, and I asked them, "Who's gonna play?" There was a piano there, and there were three seats right there at the piano, she said, "That lady over there, that's Roberta Martin. She will accompany you." I then said "Oh yes, okay," because I didn't know who Roberta Martin was. And I went there, and I said to her, I said, "Are you going to play for me?" She said, "Well, I can, yes." She said, "What are you going to sing?" I sang an old Dorsey number, one of his first, "I Claim Jesus First and That's Enough for Me." I said, "Do you know it?" She said, "No, not really, but what key do you sing it in?" "I don't know what key!" She said, "I'll tell you what you do, you start it and I'll get it."

It was almost a good fifteen, I know a good ten or fifteen minutes before they could get any kind of silence in that church. The church seats – I carried you by that church – Ebenezer right there on the corner there, it seats about 2500 people, and it was jammed, oh, so she was so amazed she didn't know what to do. She said, "Where do you live?" I told her, "I live at 3842 Langley." "Who do you live with, your parents?" I said, "Yes, my mother, father, my sisters." And she looked me up and down, do you know that before I could get home, because see I'm walking, and she's in the car, before I could get home she had been to my house, and that's where it started

When Roberta presented Eugene to the group, the other members (young boys) of the group were ecstatic to have found a new friend. Eugene stated that:

"I remember my first meeting with the Martin & Frye Quartet. Mrs. Martin had me to meet after school at her parents' house. There I met the boys: Willie, Norsalus, James and Robert. Mrs. Martin had us to rehearse the Dorsey song, Singing In My Soul. During the rehearsal, Mr. Frye dropped by and I met him. He asked Roberta to bring the group to Ebenezer that night for a singing service. That night we went to Ebenezer to sing and after singing that night, I knew that I was born to sing with Roberta Martin"

All of the singers had a uniqueness about themselves. Willie Webb's ability to play the piano was superb and James Lawrence's directorship which kept beat and timing precise. However, Eugene Smith and Norsalus McKissick's style of singing and delivery could not go untouched.

Roberta knew that she had to do something to spotlight the combined harmonies of both Eugene and Norsalus. As time progressed, the two singers: known as the "Dynamic Duo" were cleaning out churches left and right.

Roberta, seeing the success of the singing duo, had a plan that was sure to be a true "musical extravaganza". She organized a singing program and called it ***"A Singing Battle Royal: Eugene Smith vs. Norsalus McKissick"***. On that fourth Sunday night at the Ebenezer Baptist Church, in late 1934; each of the singers would sing a solo selection. Norsalus would sing, and Eugene would sing. The sing-a-thon continued until Norsalus stole the program with the gospel classic, "The Lily Of The Valley".

As he sang the lyrics to the chorus:

> ***He's a lily of the valley***
> ***He's a bright and morning star***
> ***He's the fairest of ten-thousand to my soul . . .***

the church went into a "holy ghost fit". When the smoke (spirit) had cleared, many people; including Eugene Smith and the rest of the Martin & Frye Quartet had been overtaken by the spirit of God. ***What a way to have church!!!***

In **1935**, Ms. Roberta Martin: after consulting with Prof. Frye, asked a member of the Ebenezer Baptist Church Sr. Choir if she would become a member of the Martin & Frye Quartet. Her name was **Mrs. Addie B. Smith Phillips.** Although her stay with the group would be short-lived; she was very instrumental. According to Eugene Smith, *"she was a great anthem singer."* This was a time when the Martin & Frye Quartet relied heavily on anthems as part of their repertoire. Her spotlight number was the anthem, **"Go Shepherd And Feed My Sheep"**.

In the year of **1936,** the musical career of Roberta Martin underwent a musical change. Prof. Theodore Frye left Ebenezer Bapt. Church to take over the Minister of Music duties at the Olivet Baptist Church. It was when Mr. Frye left Ebenezer for Olivet, that Roberta Martin changed the name of the group from the Martin & Frye Quartet to ***"The Roberta Martin Singers"*** – as Professor Frye gave full ownership of the group to Mrs. Roberta Martin.

Roberta Martin, like Frye, left Ebenezer Baptist Church and worshiped at her brother-in-law's church: the Shiloh Baptist Church in Inglewood, Ill., a suburb of Chicago. There she served as directress of the Choir as well as the Jr. and Youth Gospel Choruses. It was at that time that she would meet another very important person that would help to further shape and mold her life and career. That person was **Ms. Leona Price**: who in a few years would become the business manager of the Roberta Martin Studio of Gospel Music as well as Mrs. Martin's Personal Secretary.

While at the Shiloh Baptist Church, Roberta Martin once again instituted the 4th Sunday Night Musicals. On these musical extravaganzas, many great gospel singers such as: Prof. Thomas Dorsey, Sallie Martin, R.L. Knowles- who would later travel with Robert Anderson to embark on a singing crusade in California; Prof. Theodore Frye- Ms. Martin's mentor; Amelia Anderson - Ms. Martin's good friend; The Atkins Singers from Ebenezer Bapt. Church and the Roberta Martin Singers (**consisting of Eugene Smith, Norsalus McKissick, James Lawrence, Willie Webb, Robert Anderson and for a short time, W.C. Herman**) would cause sheer "fire from Heaven" to fall on the congregations of the Shiloh Bapt. Church.

In the latter part of the 1930's, the newly formed gospel music was taking distinct form and had many performers who were carrying the sound everywhere: from the street corner to every black church that would invite them. Roberta Martin would take her singers: The Roberta Martin Singers, from church to church to demonstrate this new form of religious literature. But Roberta would soon become the center of criticism by her peers. Children singing gospel songs in that era was virtually unheard of. But Roberta's love for children soon won out. Many of her peers criticized that, *"children don't know nothing about suffering and looking for a home in Heaven- they can't relate to that"*.

Roberta replied that, *"If they sing about trials and tribulations now: when that time comes- and it will come, they will know what to do and who to call upon"*. That was Roberta's theory, belief and philosophy.

In 1938, Roberta Martin and her singers: The Roberta Martin Singers – otherwise known as The Martin Gospel

Singers of Chicago were asked to carry this new gospel music to the New England and upper Northeastern United States area (Buffalo, NY, Boston, Mass., Providence, R.I., and Hartford and New Haven, Conn.): touring with gospel pioneers **Mary Johnson Davis and her husband, Professor E. Clifford Davis.** Eugene said that it was around this time that The Martin Singers first stepped into the churches of New York City to sing. They were the musical guests of Mary Johnson Davis.

It was during that time that most of the songs sung by The Roberta Martin Singers were published by the ***Roberta Martin Studio of Gospel Music***: a new music publishing house business venture owned by Roberta Martin. At the publishing house, she would make available her music to musicians, singers, composers, arrangers and choral directors: not only in the Chicago area-but all across the country. Many composers would soon send their compositions to her for her musical expertise and arrange-ability. Locally, the Roberta Martin Singers would carry sheet music into different churches - demonstrate the various parts while Roberta Martin or Willie Webb played the parts on the piano. Sheet music, at that time, was selling for 10 cents per copy. After the music was demonstrated, the group: The Roberta Martin Singers would sing the entire song. Afterwards, the members of the church choir or Gospel Chorus would buy the music, learn the song, and perform it in Sunday service. This would be the beginning of the Roberta Martin Music publishing house day to day operations.

The Roberta Martin Studio of Gospel Music was first located on 432 Bowen Avenue: which was the residence of Ms. Roberta Martin. The studio would later move to its latter day location: 69 E. 43rd Street on Chicago's Southside. Serving since its inception as manager of the Publishing House and the Personal Secretary to Mrs. Martin was Mrs. Leona Price. Roberta Martin and Leona Price worked more like sisters than business associates. It was Mrs. Price's main duty to take sheet music orders, fill the orders, mail the orders out and keep Ms. Martin updated on her daily itinerary.

Mrs. Leona Price - the manager of the Roberta Martin Studio of Gospel Music: from 1939 until her retirement in 1979. Some of the early songs composed and published by the Roberta Martin Studio of Gospel Music were:

Freedom Afterwhile (1938)
When I Wake Up In Glory- (1939)- recorded by the Ward Singers in 1950
It Is Finished (1939)

Oh, How I Love Him (1939)
The Gospel Railroad (1939)
What A Friend We Have In Jesus (1940) A Roberta Martin arrangement
If Jesus Had To Pray (1941) - recorded by Robert Anderson in 1955
Wings At The Jordan (1943)
Behold The Bridegroom Cometh (1942)
My Soul Is Satisfied (1942)
I'm Going To Follow Jesus To The End (1942)
Try Jesus, He Satisfies (1943) – first recorded by Mary Johnson Davis in '50 and later by the Roberta Martin Singers in 1960

As time progressed, Thomas Dorsey began to spend more time developing the gospel sound at the Pilgrim Baptist Church. It was in **1939** that Frye suggested to Roberta that she incorporate the musical talents of Sallie Martin: Dorsey's soloist into the group. Roberta Martin accepted Frye's suggestion and incorporated the musical talents of Sallie Martin into her group and changed the name of the group for a short time from the **"Roberta Martin Singers"** to the *"Martin and Martin Singers"*.

The Martin & Martin Singers (1939)
Front: Roberta Martin, directress and Sallie Martin,
back: Willie Webb, Robert Anderson and Eugene Smith
photo: courtesy Eugene Smith collection

Sallie Martin, already an accomplished singer/soloist with the Thomas Dorsey Singers, brought to the group, a rich deep contralto sound that she was famous for. However, the union between Sallie and Roberta was short lived as Sallie received inspiration to further her musical ministry and form her own singing group. So in 1940, Sallie Martin formed her group: *"The Sallie Martin Singers"* consisting of: **Dorothy Simmons** - who would later join Doris Akers in California to form the Akers-Simmons Duo; **Sarah Daniels - Julia Mae Smith -- Melva Williams – Ruth Jones** - pianist for the group who would later leave the group to pursue a secular music career: changing her name to the great Dinah Washington and **Cora Juanita**

Brewster – who would become Sallie's adopted daughter: Cora Juanita Martin.

The Sallie Martin Singers would receive rave notable popularity in 1944 when they were the featured singers of the legendary flamboyant female Pentecostal evangelist: Aimee Semple McPherson of Los Angeles, California.

After touring the Northeastern United States and the New England area in 1939 and early 1940; the Roberta Martin Singers were shaping and developing into an accomplished polished anointed singing unit: consisting of *Eugene Smith, Norsalus McKissick, Willie Webb, James Lawrence, Robert Anderson and Ms. Roberta Martin*. Their popularity afforded them the opportunity to sing in many churches in the Chicago and Midwestern region as they were already making a name for themselves throughout the country: partially due to their fame achieved through singing at the various National Baptist Conventions and Pentecostal Church of God in Christ Convocations in Memphis, Tenn: at the invitation of the presiding Bishop: Charles Harrison Mason.

The Roberta Martin Gospel Singers (late 1930's)
Eugene Smith, Norsalus McKissick, Willie Webb, Roberta Martin & Robert Anderson
photo courtesy of Bob Marovich – Chicago, Illinois
*this photo was taken prior to the entrance of Bessie Folk, when the group was an all-male singing group and after the disbandment of the Martin & Martin Singers

Later, in that same year of 1939; the group would undergo a new change: the formation of a "mixed group" or gospel singing group consisting of male and female vocals. Although in years prior, there were mixed singing ensembles-such as the fame Fisk Jubilee Singers; but the great efforts of Roberta brought together several young ladies of varying sounds to form an even more harmoniously sounding group of Roberta Martin Singers.

One of the earliest female singers to sing with Roberta Martin according to Eugene Smith, was a lady from the Ebenezer Baptist Church by the name of Mrs. Addie B. Phillips. This was several years before 1939 when Bessie came to the group. Addie sang with the Martin & Frye Quartet, according to Eugene Smith, during a time when the Martin & Frye Quartet were in their infant stages and singing mostly anthems. As Eugene stated:

> ***Lord, Addie could take an anthem, such as the song "Go Shepherd and Feed My Sheep" or "Listen To The Lambs" and literally kill you. Lord knows what would have happened if she had kept on singing with us.***

The first real historically authenticated female singer within the Roberta Martin Singers was Bessie Folk. Bessie Folk, a petite brown skinned lady, was a star member of a group called, **"The Stepsie Five".** This group came out of the Canaan Baptist Church where Rev. Lewis Rawls was the pastor. During that time, she was often referred to as "Little Mahalia": due in part to her rich vocal qualities and youthful ability to belt out a song..

Bessie Folk

When Roberta heard her sing, she was so thrilled with her ability and spirit that after a period of time had passed, she asked her mother if Bessie could become a member of the group. Bessie's parents were so thrilled with the offer for Bessie to be trained by Roberta Martin that they readily approved of the request. Thus in early **1939**, Bessie Folk became a member of The Roberta Martin Singers. Although she was elated to becoming a member of the Roberta Martin Singers, at first, she met some opposition from the male members. Mrs. Martin had trained and rehearsed Bessie before taking her to sing in Baltimore, Maryland. When the boys saw who Mrs. Martin had brought, it was met with stern opposition.

As Eugene stated, *"it wasn't that we did not like her; it was just that we were all so close knit and we weren't ready for someone else to come into our close knit family".* Mrs. Martin told the boys, *"If you boys don't want Bessie to sing, that's fine. I'll take Bessie and we'll go back to Chicago".* The boys wouldn't have that. Bessie sang with the group and within a very short period of time, a strong brotherly-sisterly sibling love developed. ***"Bessie was not only a Martin Singer; she was our little sister".*** Bessie would soon become a star singer within the group with the recording of her most famous selection, ***"Only A Look".*** That song would become the signature theme song of the group in later years.

Prior to the 1940's; some of the popular songs of The Martin & Frye Quartet and later The Roberta Martin Singers were:

1934 – Talk About A Chile That Do Love Jesus
1936 – Go Shephard & Feed My Sheep
1937 – Going Back To Jesus
1938- Walk In Jerusalem (a jubilistic version)
1939 – The Gospel Railroad
1939 – It Is Finished – Roberta Martin's Easter masterpiece

The 1940's

The Roberta Martin Singers
"establishing their trademark sound & embarking on a recording career"

L to r: Eugene Smith, Bessie Folk, Delois Barrett, Norsalus McKissick – Roberta Martin in front

In February **1941**, Roberta Martin and her singers were invited to bring this new music to the West Coast of America. They were brought to California under the promotion of the late, Rev. Arthur Peters: pastor of the Victory Baptist Church in Los Angeles. Leaving from Chicago, the group was scheduled to sing nightly for one week. However, due to the thunderous singing power of the Roberta Martin Singers, they were in California for more than seven (7) weeks.

During their many visits California, the Martin Singers graced West Coast churches with such selections as:

1. *Don't Wonder About Him*
2. *Stretch Out In These Dark Hours of Distress*
3. *He Will Carry You Through (Yield Not To Temptation)*
4. *The Old Ship of Zion*
5. *The Unclouded Day*
6. *The Angels Are Hovering Round*

Eugene Smith once told of an incident which happened when the Roberta Martin Singers went to California. As Eugene Smith retold the story in an interview with Bob Marovich:

And we hit that air one Sunday night, I think our program was Monday. I know the black people was looking for something different, the style of music and everything was just different...and we hit that air with "Jesus," and the next day the people instead of getting off, instead of going home from work, they would come to the church early to get a seat. And that is when Ethel Waters and all of the popular Hollywood stars were there. They kind of thought that by being celebrities, they spoke. And so Rev. Branham would have them get up, you know, "Look who's here, Louise Beavers, come on up here!" And I never will forget what Hattie McDaniels said, "I heard that boy sing and I want to see who that person was that was calling Jesus." And that was me!

That thunderous visit led the Roberta Martin Singers to annually visit California for many years afterwards. Soon, their evangelistic schedule carried the Martin Singers to Florida and the Deep South throughout the winter months: in order to escape the harsh winters in the Midwest and the East.

Eugene stated:

Yeah, we would leave here (Chicago) in January, about this time now, we would go maybe to Miami, Jacksonville, in Florida and some of the southern states but mostly Florida one year, and the next year would be California, Oakland, San Francisco, Los Angeles. All around. And we would be there until around April, March, latter part of March, and then come home in April. We had an engagement for 30 years from Palm Sunday to Easter Sunday. We'd see people bring their children in the cradle and see them grow up and have children following the Martins. (Bob Marovich interview)

Later in that same year, Eugene Smith would compose his only and most famous composition, **"I Know The Lord Will Make a Way, Yes He Will"**. That song would be published by the Martin Studio of Gospel Music and later recorded by the group on Apollo Records with Myrtle Scott as lead.

Eugene Smith

(sheet music printed, permission courtesy of Leonard Austin)

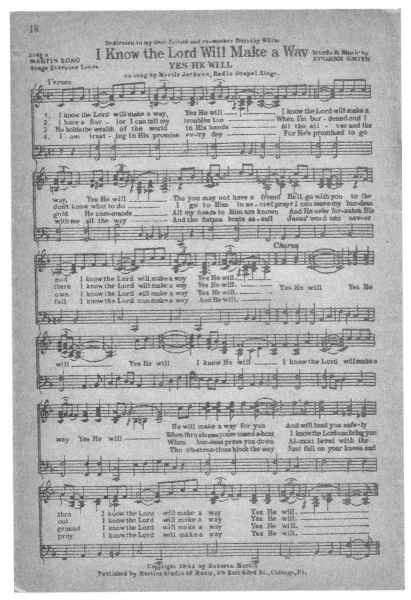

In October, 1941; the Roberta Martin Singers were the musical guest at the Psalmist Baptist Church; pastored by Rev. Julius Gray in Maryland. While there, they performed an informal recital for Mayor Jackson and other city officials.

While on the East Coast, the Roberta Martin Singers would introduce a song and that song would help launch the career of both the Roberta Martin Singers and the Roberta Martin Studio of Gospel Music. The song, written by the late Phyllis Hall: a former orphan who sang the The Martin Singers was entitled; **"He Knows Just How Much We Can Bear"**. Eugene retold me the story of how that song came into being:

> *"We were summoned to the White Rock Bapt. Church in Philadelphia for a week's revival. On that first night, a young Phyllis Hall came and sang the song. After service, she gave the song to Roberta Martin for her to give it the Martin touch. Roberta rearranged the song and taught it to us. When we sang the song on Wednesday night, the response was sheer spiritual excitement. That song tore up the place. " That was in late 1941. She (Phyllis Hall) then sang with us for a brief time in the latter part of 1941 and early 1942 whenever we were in the Philadelphia-Baltimore area."*

In early **1943**, Norsalus McKissick: a leading member of the group; was directing the choir at the Central Baptist Church in Chicago. In the choir was a young Delois Barrett. She had a unique soprano voice which prompted Norsalus to tell Roberta about her. When Roberta Martin heard her sing, she was truly amazed at her voice, quality and range.

Delois Barrett Campbell
Soprano

Roberta quickly invited her to sing in the group. But once again, Roberta had to receive the permission from Delois's parents. After receiving their blessings, Roberta, for the next few years, trained Delois: writing songs for her and tailoring them to her already polished vocal quality. Roberta would then spend time training both Delois and Bessie's voices: teaching them how to create a sound that could only be duplicated in Heaven.

Roberta Martin, being the great singer, songstress, composer and arranger that she was, instructed and encouraged her singers not to holler or scream when singing. Instead, she taught them total vocal control and how to take a song and paint a picture to the audience.

Eugene Smith said that *"when Delois went with the Martin Singers to California, she tore up California with "Yield Not To Temptation. That song nearly killed Prof. J. Earle Hines".*

Roberta later recorded **"Yield Not To Temptation"** on a vanity recording for Religious Records of Detroit, Michigan in 1947 with Delois on lead. That selection was also released as **"He Will Carry You Through"**. Many other groups would hear that selection and later record it with their own arrangement: including Prof. J. Earle Hines and the St. Paul Baptist Church choir of Los Angeles in 1947- who heard the Roberta Martin Singers sing the selection prior to their recording of the tune; Martin Singers alumnus Myrtle Jackson in 1951 and Margaret Allison & The Angelic Gospel Singers of Philadelphia in 1970.

In **1943,** Eugene Smith was drafted into the army. This was the only time in the history of the Roberta Martin Singers that Eugene Smith was not a part of the singing entourage. But in the absence of "Gene"; the remaining singers: ***Roberta, Norsalus, Bessie, Delois, and Willie Webb*** would carry on the great Roberta Martin sound. After serving in the United States Army for only nine months and receiving an honorable discharge for being short in stature, Eugene was sent back to Chicago and continued his gospel singing with the Roberta Martin Singers. As Gene returned home to continue singing songs of Zion; Norsalus McKissick departed for "Uncle Sam's" army. This time, a member of the Martin Singers would serve active duty the entire four year term.

In the latter part of **1943**, Roberta Martin's singing and traveling schedule and her devotion to the music publishing house caused her to curtail her involvement at the National Baptist Convention held in Chicago. Although she was a part of the massive religious gathering, she endorsed one of her students: Robert Anderson, to substitute for her as a convention soloist. He chose to sing the song, "Something Within Me", written by Mrs.Lucie Campbell- musical matriarch of the National Baptist Convention. When Robert finished the song, he literally tore up the convention.

The Martin Singers were the masters of carrying messages in song. One such song, ***"In These Dark Hours of Distress",*** also known: as Eugene called it- ***"Stretch Out";*** became one of the songs that the Martin Singers sang all across the United States during the time of ***World War II: from 1942-1944.*** There were so many families in so many church congregations that were affected by the war with so many fathers, sons, uncles, cousin, grandfathers, etc., fighting that the comfort that most people got were from the words of the song . . . . .

Oh Lord, we come now - as humble as we know how
With our hearts laying bear - as before thee we bow
Dark clouds, hover over us - and nowhere is
there rest

Lord, only thee can save us-in these dark hours of distress
Let us stretch out, on thy word - Til thy comforting voice be heard
Lord give us strength to go onward - In these dark hours, of distress . . . . .

*That song consoled many families through those terrible times and it was bellowed across the country by Eugene Smith and The Martin Singers

Recording made in Hollywood, California
* according to Eugene Smith, recording RIH #101 was made when the Roberta Martin Singers ventured back to California in 1945. However, book sources have this recording session as 1949. According to Eugene Smith, the following personnel were present at that session: Roberta Martin-pianist, Willie Webb-organist, Norsalus McKissick, Delois Barrett, Bessie Folk, Eugene Smith and Sadie Durrah.

RIH #101 Only A Look - led by Bessie Folk
Jesus - led by Eugene Smith

Eugene Smith, commonly called, **"The Boy Wonder gospel singer";** was always said to have been the backbone of the group. Singing, and later recording countless selections; one of his early career favorite's was the song "God Leads His Dear Children Along". Although never recording the selection; right out of the army, Eugene, and the Roberta Martin Singers took this song- "God Leads His

Dear Children Along" . . . . . to many, many churches and church congregations including the now historic Masonic Temple in St. Louis, Missouri.

"In shady green pastures, so rich and so sweet
God leads, his dear children, along
Where the waters, cool flow; bathe the weary ones feet
God leads, his dear children, along"

"Some through the waters, some through the flood
Some through the fire, but all through the blood
Some through great sorrows, but God gives a song
In the night season, and all the day long . . . . ."

They were invited to the city of St. Louis, Missouri to a massive gospel program in **1944** by gospel music pioneer: Madame Willie Mae Ford Smith. When Gene and the singers finished singing that selection, as Mde. Willie Mae Ford Smith stated, "It was time to go home."

Also during the mid 1940's; Eugene sang and later recorded another song, **"No, No, Nothing Can Change Me"** - written by the late Henry J. Ford and arranged by Roberta Martin. This song was recorded on the Martin Studio of Gospel Music label in 1947 and once again, carried the signature Eugene Smith style.

As the late Rev. James Cleveland once stated **"He was the first man in gospel music that coined the term "showman". That term was used to describe a person who** *would sing and could not keep still"*. He could literally take a song and with gestures and movements, paint a virtual picture of the song. In the 1940's, Roberta Martin wrote and arranged a song especially for Eugene entitled, **"Don't Wonder About Him"**. Although Eugene and the group "wore out" many churches with that selection; it was his earlier composition: "I Know The Lord Will Make A Way, Yes He Will" which would catapult Eugene into the spotlight as a prolific gospel songwriter. Many times, when the Martin Gospel Singers would sing these two and many other songs; as Eugene would put it: *"it was pure doxology"*. As Bessie stated once: *"we were in Ft. Worth, Texas and Eugene sang Don't Wonder About Him and ran all around that church" All we could do was keep on singing as the folk were shouting-left and right"*.

1945 brought a new spark of energy to the already anointed Roberta Martin Singers as ***Mrs. Sadie Durrah-Nolan*** joined and became a part of the great gospel entourage. Sadie, a rich contralto singer was a member of the same church as Eugene Smith: the Salem Baptist Church and also served as the director of the New Mount Olive Baptist Church Gospel Chorus. Sadie soon became a premiere soloist of the group: partly because of her unique quality and style for delivering such musical classics as: "Move On Up A Little Higher" :the song that made Mahalia Jackson a household name, "I'm Bound For Canaan Land", "I Have A Friend Above All Others", "Down On My Knees", and **"There's Not A Friend Like Jesus"** the only song she recorded with the Martin Singers where she was spotlighted as lead soloist.

Although her death in 1947 was untimely, she did not receive the gospel recognition that was due her.

The Roberta Martin Singers - 1946
Front: Norsalus McKissick, Sadie Durrah, Bessie Folk, Eugene Smith
Back: Roberta Martin, Willie Webb, Delois Barrett Campbell
Photo: *courtesy Leonard Austin collection*
*** Mrs. Sadie Durrah- Nolan (1946)*
recorded ***"There's Not A Friend Like Jesus"*** *with the Roberta Martin Singers in 1947 on Fidelity Records*
*on the flip side of that recording was "Don't Wonder 'Bout Him" led by Eugene Smith
Photo: courtesy of Leonard Austin

As Eugene stated about Sadie:

'we were singing at Tabernacle Baptist Church at a program in January, 1946 and Sadie was leading Move On Up A Little Higher". There was a snowstorm outside, but Lord was it hot in that church. When Sadie really began to stretch out on the song, someone screamed and said, "sang it Sadie". When I looked and saw who it was, it was Mahalia Jackson. Mahalia shouted all over that church after Sadie wore that song out."

From 1940-1946; the Martin Singers were true gospel spokespersons: singing from one end of America to the other. During that time; some of the popular songs of the Roberta Martin Singers: sung in churches, revivals and denominational conventions prior to their recording debut were as follows:

1941 – I Heard The Voice of Jesus Say- popular Roberta Martin solo

1942- Behold The Bride Groom Cometh
I'm Going To Heaven Anyhow

1943- Wings At The Jordan
My Soul IS Satisfied
The Storm Is Passing Over, Hallelujah
Try Jesus, He Satisfies
God Leads His Dear Children Along

1944- I Will Trust Thee, Lord
       Lord, I Won't Turn Back
       The Angels Are Hovering Round
       Have You Any Witness In Your Heart
       When I Get Home
       That Is Why, My Soul IS Free

1945- I'm Bound For Higher Ground

1946- This Same Jesus
       Mother's Voice

****The previous selections were a compilation of songs sung by the Martin Singers and chosen by Eugene Smith, Bessie Folk, Delois Barrett Campbell and Little Lucy Smith after going through a number of Roberta Martin Singer's songbooks: which dates back to the earliest pieces of music published by the Roberta Martin Studio of Gospel Music in 1938.** Song titles by permission from Leonard Austin.*

1947 was a banner year for the Roberta Martin Singers as they were embarking upon a new venue: gospel recording artist. Although they had been singing for fourteen years: since 1933 and had previously made a recording on their trip to California; these series of pilot recordings on a label called **Fidelity Records** would serve as the launching pad for a successful upcoming recording career for Apollo and later, Savoy Records.

The personnel for this recording session in Chicago in 1947 were as follows:

Roberta Martin, Contralto & Pianist
Willie Webb, Baritone & Organist
Delois Barrett, Soprano
Sadie Durrah-Nolan, Alto
Bessie Folk, Contralto
Norsalus McKissick, Tenor
Eugene Smith, Baritone

Out of that session came the first set of professional recordings for The Roberta Martin Singers: two on the Fidelity label and one on the Religious Recordings of Detroit label.

Fidelity Records:

#2000   Precious Memories - led by Norsalus McKissick (1947)

He's All I Need - led by Eugene Smith (1947)

#2003   Don't Wonder About Him - led by Eugene Smith (1947)

There's Not A Friend Like Jesus-led by Saddie Durrah (1947)

Religious Recordings of Detroit, Michigan

Pass Me Not, Oh Gentle Saviour –led by Eugene Smith (1947) *not issued
Nothing Can Change Me – led by Eugene Smith (1947)
Yield Not To Temptation – led by Delois Barrett (1947)
Didn't It Rain – led by Roberta Martin (1947)

Madame Willie Mae Ford Smith
Photo: courtesy of Chicago Public
Library - Lucy Collier collection
She and Roberta Martin were close friends and both were
officers in the Thomas Dorsey Gospel Music Convention:
The National Convention of Gospel Choirs and Choruses

The many faces of the Lucy Smith Singers

Lucy Smith Singers
Gladys Beamon, Katherine Campbell,
Sarah McKissick & Little Lucy Smith
Courtesy: Chicago Public Library - Lucy Collier collection

The Lucy Smith Singers early 1940's
Catherine Campbell, Little Lucy Smith, Gladys Beamon
Courtesy: Chicago Public Library – Lucy Collier collection

The Lucy Smith Singers (mid 1940's)
Gladys Beamon, Little Lucy Smith, Sarah
McKissick, Catherine Campbell
Courtesy: Chicago Public library- Lucy Collier collection

Lucy began playing at the age of six, singing on the weekly radio broadcast of the All Nations Pentecostal Church. One of Lucy's big radio selections was **"Tell Jesus All"**. When "little" Lucy would sing the song, the church would go up into a holy ghost frenzy. Lucy would ask a question:

Are you burdened, worn and weary
Heeding still, the Master's call
If in your life, each day is dreary
Just tell Jesus, tell Jesus all . . . . .

When Lucy would finish singing the verse, the choir would assist her in the chorus. Hearing Little Lucy create those up in the rafter yells, one would become bewildered at the marvel of her vocal and phrasing techniques.

In the month of August, **1947**; the Roberta Martin Singers were rehearsing for their yearly anniversary at the old Great Coliseum in Chicago. Their guest for the fourteenth celebration would be Mother Willie Mae Ford Smith of St. Louis, Rev. Clarence Cobbs and the First Church of Deliverance choir; and the Lucy Smith Trio: consisting of "Little" Lucy Smith, Gladys Beamon and Florine Watson. The Lucy Smith Singers later added the talents of Sarah McKissick Simmons and Katherine Campbell after Florine Watson left the group. It was during that time that Lucy decided to devise a plan on how to play matchmaker for her father and Roberta Martin. Eugene stated how Little Lucy Smith played matchmaker for the unsuspecting couple:

> *"Lucy: knowing that her father was at home, asked Roberta Martin if she would drive her home after rehearsal. Roberta agreed and after rehearsal, she drove Lucy home: then located on Ellis Avenue and 37th Street. When they arrived at the house, Lucy invited Roberta Martin inside to meet her father. After meeting each other, a brief engagement occurred. That engagement led to the marriage of Roberta Evelyn Martin to Mr. James "Jimmy" Austin on December 31, 1947 at the home of Roberta Martin, located on South Michigan Avenue."*

5430 So. Michigan Ave.
the residence of Mrs. Roberta Martin during the 1940's. 5430 South Michigan Avenue was the first residence where Leonard "Sonny" Austin called home

Both Photos: courtesy Leonard Austin collection

The wedding photo of James & Roberta Martin Austin December 31, 1947
Photo: Leonard Austin collection

SMITH JUBILEE SINGERS.

HOME ADDRESS,
3733 VINCENNES AVE.,
CHICAGO, ILL.

Photo: courtesy of the Chicago Public Library
From the Lucy Smith Collier collection

Professional photograph: takes during late 1920's of the Lucy Smith Jubilee Singers of the All Nations Pentecostal Church. They recorded two cylinders (early forms of records): ***Seeking For Me and No Room At The Hotel***. Notice the little girl in the front is "Little" Lucy Smith. The gentleman back left is Little Lucy's father: Jimmie Austin – who later married Roberta Martin on December 31, 1947.

1947 would also test the faith of the Roberta Martin Singers as they said goodbye to group member, **"Mrs. Sadie Durrah-Nolan"** who passed away shortly after recording the selection, "There's Not a Friend like Jesus". All of the members of the group were saddened and deeply touched at the loss of Sadie, but knew that she lived the life that she sang about. As Eugene reminisced:

"We all went into a deep depression when Sadie died. It happened so sudden. Although she was older than any of us, we just felt that she would go on and on" replied Gene. I really think Roberta took it the hardest."

In **1948**, after hearing those vintage recordings of the Roberta Martin Singers on local radio; a record label owner, Bess Berman, owner of the Apollo Recording Company in New York City; asked Roberta Martin if she and her singers would record some gospel music on her Apollo Recording label. The only other gospel artist on Apollo Records at that time was fellow Chicagoan, Mahalia Jackson.

After agreeing to record for Apollo Records; this recording label would launch some of the greatest Roberta Martin Singers gospel recordings ever: which span a timeframe from 1949-1956. During that time span; Roberta Martin and her singers: The Roberta Martin Singers, recorded 44 selections for Apollo Records and showcased the singing talents of several lead singers including:

Eugene Smith – which led 19 selections

Norsalus McKissick – which led 11 selections
Delois Barrett – which led 5 selections
Bess Folk – which led 3 selections
Myrtle Scott – which led 3 selections
Myrtle Jackson – which led 1 selection
Even Roberta Martin herself led 7 selections

On many of the Apollo recordings, the following selections were shared by two or more leaders including:

Where Can I Go – Roberta Martin and Myrtle Scott
He Didn't Mind Dying – Roberta Martin & Myrtle Jackson
After It's All Over – Roberta Martin & Eugene Smith
Let God Abide – Eugene Smith & Norsalus McKissick
I'm Determined – Eugene Smith & Norsalus McKissick
He's Using Me – Eugene Smith & Norsalus McKissick
Do You Know Jesus – Eugene Smith & Roberta Martin

In **1949**, Bessie Folk, the first female singer with the group, recorded the legendary song, written by the late Mrs. Anna Shepherd and published by the Martin Studio of Gospel Music: **ONLY A LOOK**. That song had become the theme song of the Roberta Martin Singers during the mid 1940's. However, long before the Roberta Martin Singers began singing Only A Look; the theme song of the

Martin & Frye Quartet was ***"Is Your All On The Altar"***- which they sang into the 1940's. Although Apollo Records popularized the selection, the Roberta Martin Singers first recorded "Only A Look" in California on their vintage R.I.H. Records: again with Bessie Folk as the leader.

Norsalus McKissick, recently returning from the US Army, recorded a famous Thomas Dorsey composition, "The Old Ship of Zion", with a Roberta Martin arrangement. These songs were so popular within the African American community, that both selections afforded the Roberta Martin Singers the first two of several Gold Records they would receive.

Eventhough the list of gospel songs by the Martin Singers seemed endless; another important song in the career of the Roberta Martin Singers was the stirring: **"He Know How Much We Can Bear"**. This song was recorded twice: first for Apollo Records where Roberta Martin takes a slow yet strong and soul stirring approach to the lead on the song and the latter recording on Savoy Records- with a Lucy Smith arrangement- where the group lays down a smooth background to Mrs. Martin's still strong and soul stirring lead. Both times, the followers of the Roberta Martin Singers were stirred when they heard the selection.

Eugene Smith foretold of how that song came about:

"Back in those days, in about the late 1938's- after the founding of the Roberta Martin Publishing House, Roberta would carry us from Choir

rehearsal to choir rehearsal, to those churches who would let us in. We would demonstrate the music as the Gospel Choirs and Choruses would catch on to what we were doing and introducing other numbers. Time went on and on and on and seemed like a very slow pace. But we were just grateful to get on the inside of churches to introduce the music that today is called GOSPEL. And one day this tune was written, by a young lady named Phyllis Hall —who had been an orphan and lived to tell of her experiences. From the time that the song was written until presently, we never had to look back. We are our Heavenly Father's children, and we all know, that he loves us one and all. Yet there are times when we find an answer to another's voice and call. But if we are willing, the Lord will teach us. His voice only, to obey no matter where. For he knows, just, how much, we can bear.

Roberta Martin Singers tidbit:

* This came from a 1994 interview that Gospel historian Linwood Heath of Philadelphia had with the late great Francis Steadman of the Famous Ward Singers and the Stars of Faith . . . .

According to the late Frances Steadman, lead singer of the Famous Ward Singers and the Stars of Faith, the Roberta Martin Singers first went to Baltimore to sing in the early 1940's- around 1945. The first Martin Singers group she saw was the group that consisted of **Roberta, Robert Anderson, Willie Webb, Eugene Smith and Norsalus McKissick.** When she heard them, the first song that they sang at that time was not "Only A Look", but **"Is Your All On The Altar".**

The second time they came to Baltimore, she had all the male singers except Robert Anderson and a female singer: Bessie Folk. The third time the Roberta Martin Singers came to Baltimore, she had a lady that reminded you of Madame Henrietta Waddy of the Ward Singers singing with her by the name of Sadie Durrah. Now we are talking about 1946 or 1947.

According to Frances, "Roberta Martin came back to Baltimore year after year with the group. During that time, I saw such the Roberta Martin Singers with such singers as Myrtle Scott, Myrtle Jackson and Delois Barrett. Even Mary Johnson Davis and yes, Clara Ward sang in Baltimore with the Roberta Martin Singers- *and I wouldn't have believed it if I had not seen it for myself".*

Frances recalls one of the last times that Frances saw the Roberta Martin Singers in Baltimore. "They were singing and about midway the program, Eugene Smith told that audience of a lady that sang briefly with them was in the area and would sing with them on that night. That night, the great **DINAH WASHINGTON** sang in Baltimore with the Roberta Martin Singers and led the song, "He Knows My Heart" as the Martin Singers backgrounds her and Roberta Martin played the piano and Willie Webb played the organ.

Dr. Stanley Keeble, a key founding component of the Gospel Music Museum in Chicago told me that the late Rev. James Cleveland purchased his first car from Mrs. Roberta Martin. She had, in turn, purchased the same car from Willie Webb. *"Seems like music was not the only thing that they kept within the stable of Mrs. Roberta Martin".*

Eugene Smith shared a Roberta Martin moment. *He stated, "we were invited to sing at the Apollo Theater in New York City. I eagerly asked Roberta if we could go sing at the Apollo". She stated, "Gene, you may get a group together and take the Eugene Smith Singers to the Apollo, but the Roberta Martin Singers will not go to the Apollo Theater."* She did not believe in carrying the church into worldly places.

The following are some of the important dates in the early career (1933-1948) of Roberta Martin and The Roberta Martin Singers

1934 The Youth Department of the National Convention of Gospel Choirs and Choruses was added at the meeting in St. Louis. Ms. Roberta Martin was elected as National Supervisor.

1936 (June) at the National Baptist Sunday School Congress in New Orleans; Roberta Martin, Robert Anderson and Eugene Smith (age 14) were part of the delegation which included Rev. J.H.Lorenzo Smith, Prof. Theodore R. Frye, Mrs. Cordelia Frye, Camille Ellis, Eldora Robinson.

Mrs. Roberta Martin and Sallie Martin battled in a "Song Battle" sponsored by Prof. Thomas Dorsey. It is said to be the first gospel program that charged a fee instead of a love offering.

1938 Pilgrim Baptist Church and 1st Church of Deliverance jointly sponsored a "Song Battle" between Roberta Martin and Sallie Martin at DuSable High School.

1939 (Brooklyn, NY) - The Roberta Martin Singers closed out with a thunderous response at the National Convention of Gospel Choirs and Choruses.

(December 31-Chicago) Roberta Martin sang on the Watch Meeting service at Pilgrim Baptist Church along with Sallie Martin and the famed Wings Over Jordan

1941 (May) - Roberta Martin and her singers rendered a special program at the 2nd Baptist Church in Middletown, Ill.

(October) – The Roberta Martin Singers and the Lux Singers of Chicago were in a spiritually charged "Song Battle".

1942 The Roberta Martin Singers were in Philadelphia at the Mt. Zion Baptist Church: pastored by the Rev. J. Timothy Boddie: The members present were Roberta Martin, Eugene Smith, Norsalus McKissick, James Lawrence, Robert Anderson and Phyllis Hall.

The Roberta Martin Singers sang on a program for The Lux Singers at the Chicago YMCA on State Street.

1943 (June) - The Roberta Martin Singers celebrated the 21st Anniversary of Prof. Thomas A. Dorsey. Other guests included Sis. Willie Mae Ford Smith, the Pilgrim Gospel Chorus, Theodore R. Frye; the Olivet Trio, the Martin-Morris Singers, Mahalia Jackson, Myrtle Jackson, Herman Clay, Pauline Phelps, the Hamilton Singers and Magnolia Lewis Butts

(November) - Miss Roberta Martin sings at the opening musical of the 63rd National Baptist Convention at the 8th Regiment Armory in Chicago.

1944 The Roberta Martin Singers sang at the 1st Church of Deliverance Candle Light Service at Comisky Park along with Chicago soloist: Elizabeth Hall.

1946 Roberta Martin and Mahalia Jackson squared off in a "Song Battle" at the Tabernacle Baptist Church on August 18. Also on the program were Myrtle Scott, Sallie Martin and Robert Anderson.

1947 The Roberta Martin Singers made their first professional recordings. Also in that same year, Ms. Roberta Evelyn Martin marries Mr. James "Jimmy" Austin: the father of "Little" Lucy Smith. Sadie Durrah-Nolan passed away.

1948 (March) - Mrs. Roberta Martin Austin: then a newlywed, was the special guest at the Ebenezer Bapt. Church Usher Board's 10th Annual Tea at Poro College.

1948 (September) - The Roberta Martin Singers were special guest at the National Baptist Convention in Houston, Texas: along with Prof. Theodore Frye, Mahalia Jackson, the Famous Ward Singers from Philadelphia and Martha Bass from St. Louis

After an extremely spiritual series of performances at the **1948** National Baptist Convention in Houston Texas; along with other gospel greats Mahalia Jackson and the Famous Ward Singers; the Roberta Martin Singers were considered the number #1 premier gospel singing group in the circles of African American sacred music and especially the Black church. That was about to skyrocket even more as they were about to begin recording for a new venture: Apollo Records of New York City.

During the month of July in the year of **1949**, the Roberta Martin Singers completed their first recording session for Apollo Records in New York City. In that session, **Roberta Martin** carried the lead as pianist and contralto. The remaining singers: **Norsalus McKissick, Bessie Folk, Delois Barrett and Eugene Smith** assumed their roles as background singers and featured soloist. Also in that session, **"Little" Lucy Smith**, the step daughter of Roberta Martin and leader of the Lucy Smith Trio served as organist- accompanying Roberta Martin: her new step-mother.

From that session, the following recordings were produced:

Apollo Records: - July, 1949
My Friend - Delois Barrett   Apollo #218
I'll Follow In His Footsteps - Eugene Smith   Apollo #249
Only A Look - Bessie Folk   Apollo #214
He Knows How Much We Can Bear - Roberta Martin   Apollo #214
The Old Ship of Zion - Norsalus McKissick   Apollo #223
What A Blessing In Jesus I Found - Delois Barrett   Apollo #218

This series of gospel recordings helped to create an avenue that would launch the career for the Roberta Martin Singers and carry them to many cities and churches not yet explored by the singing evangelists. Two of these early recordings: Only A Look and The Old Ship of Zion would later afford the Roberta Martin Singers a series of honorary awards.

Also in **1949**, a young Romance Watson became a member of the Roberta Martin Singers. Romance, then a member of the All Nations Pentecostal Church, pastored by the late Elder Lucy Smith: an early prominent female pastor in the city of Chicago; lived behind Mrs. Martin's residence on Bowen Avenue. It was a real thrill each and every afternoon for Romance to be playing in his backyard : only to see Mrs. Martin drive her Cadillac into her driveway. He would yell, "hello Mrs. Martin". She would reply, "Hello Romance- how is your family?" That was the beginning of a beautiful relationship. Romance, along with his family The Watson Singers: consisting of sisters Florine and Sylvia Watson would sing on the radio broadcast of the All Nations Church: along with Little Lucy Smith, Elder Smith's granddaughter. While singing and traveling with the family group,"The Watson Singers"; Eugene Smith called him and told him that Roberta Martin wanted to talk to him. When he went to visit Mrs. Martin, she asked him if he would like to become a member of the group. Romance; overjoyed and thrilled; readily accepted the invitation and became a member of the famed Roberta Martin Singers.

Romance first traveled with the group to Philadelphia, Pennsylvania to the Mount Carmel Baptist Church; pastored by the late Rev. D.W. Hoggard. It was at that church that Romance fell in love with the pastor's daughter and she soon became his wife. Romance loved Philadelphia so much that after his stay with the Martin Singers, he made Philadelphia his permanent residence. Although Romance sang with the group during the golden era of the 1950's; it was not until 1957 that he is heard taking a solo lead on recordings with the signature song, **"When He Sets Me Free"** and on a duet with Norsalus McKissick singing the Doris Akers classic, **"God Is So Good To Me".**

Also in that same year of 1949, Roberta Martin began focusing more on writing, arranging and composing songs at the Roberta Martin Studio of Gospel Music. It was then that she decided to place the management aspects of the Martin Singers into the capable hands of Eugene Smith: one of the original members. Eugene would then begin to take over the day to day aspects of managing the Roberta Martin Singers: from booking Evangelistic /Revival meetings to filing singing vacancies. Mrs. Martin would still remain the ultimate decision maker. She would, in later years, turn that role of music director and arranger over to Little Lucy Smith.

Although the Martin Singers were singing musical masterpieces nightly such as Only A Look, The Old Ship of Zion and He Knows How Much We Can Bear; several selections performed "in person" by the Martin Singers and published by the Martin Studio were sung and recorded by various other artists including:

I've Got To Cross Over (1949)– known as Get Away Jordan – which was recorded by the Famous Ward Singers and later by The Gospel Harmonettes.

Each Day, I Grow A Little Nearer (1948) – later recorded by Clara Ward and Marion Williams and the Famous Ward Singers

The Unclouded Day – (1939) – later recorded by The Staple Singers

Every Day, Every Hour – (1950) – an arrangement of the old hymn was recorded by Alex Bradford and the Willie Webb Singers

God Will Take Care – (1951) – recorded by the Gay Sisters of Chicago.

He'll Never Let Go Your Hand- (1951) – recorded by The Clara Ward Special.

The Roberta Martin Singers
In service

Bessie Folk and Eugene Smith encourage Norsalus McKissick as Mrs. Martin is to the left of Norsalus.
Photo: courtesy of Leonard Austin collection

Unidentified man, Mrs. Martin (back center), unidentified woman Little Lucy Smith, Eugene Smith
Photo: courtesy Leonard Austin collection

Roberta Martin and Eugene Smith
Photo: courtesy Leonard Austin collection

"Chicago's Great Musicians"
*Roberta Martin (at Piano) sitiing beside Robert Anderson
Behind Robert Anderson is Willie Webb
Next to Robert Anderson is a young Edward Robinson
In front of Edward Robinson is Ralph Goodpasteur
This picture was taken at the First
Church of Deliverance, Chicago
Photo: courtesy Eugene Smith collection*

The 1950's

The Roberta Martin Singers
"setting the standard – raising the bar"

In January, 1950; the Roberta Martin Singers were back at the studios of Apollo Records in New York City to once again record a series of religious masterpieces. At that 1950 session, the groups personnel remained the same as singers Eugene Smith, Norsalus McKissick, Bessie Folk and Delois Barrett were musically assisted by Roberta Martin on Piano and Little Lucy Smith on the Organ. That session produced the following six selections:

Do You Know Him - Eugene Smith	Apollo #223
Tell Jesus All - Bessie Folk	Apollo #249
Let It Be - Delois Barrett	Apollo #238
Satisfied - Eugene Smith	Apollo #227
What A Friend We Have In Jesus - Roberta Martin	Apollo #238
My Eternal Home - Norsalus McKissick	Apollo #227

The era of the 1950's also saw the birth of many great songs at the Roberta Martin Studio of Gospel Music. Many writers began submitting their songs to the Roberta Martin Studio for that special "Roberta Martin Touch".

A young Alex Bradford, from Birmingham, Alabama would have a great musical foundational molding by the hands of a Roberta Martin disciple: Willie Webb. Alex; the son of Olivia Bradford Spain, attended the Baptist Church and later the Sanctified or the Holiness Church. After finishing high school and Army training, he first moved to New York and then to Chicago. It was there in Chicago that he met Roberta Martin.

Prof. Alex Bradford
Photo: courtesy Eugene Smith collection

Eugene Smith recalls when Alex Bradford first met Roberta Martin.

"Alex Bradford came to Mrs. Martin's house at 5430 So. Michigan Ave.. When he rang the door bell, I answered the door. He said, hello, I am Alex Bradford from Birmingham. I replied, hello, I'm Eugene Smith. Alex went crazy after meeting me (Eugene). He said he wanted to meet Mrs. Martin and bring her some songs to listen to. When Mrs. Martin came to meet him, once again, he was in sheer shock. After playing and singing some of his songs, she took the songs and told Alex to come to her studio and the rest in gospel history.

Mrs. Martin took those songs... written by Alex Bradford; and recorded them with the Martin Singers on the Apollo label. Those selections were:

1. There A Man On The Other Side of Jordan
2. Come In The Room
3. Since I Met Jesus
4. After It's All Over
5. Too Close To Heaven

When the countless number of people all across the nation heard those songs; not only were the Martin Singers in greater demand for revivals and concerts, but Alex Bradford became one of the most sought after songwriters in gospel music.

Alex had high aspirations of singing with the Martin Singers, but according to Eugene Smith, **"we had a full roster - there was no room for him at the time"**. Alex then began singing with the Willie Webb Singers. Willie was another "original" member of the Martin-Frye Quartet and the Roberta Martin Singers. He first recorded the gospel arrangement of the hymn "Savior More Than Life To Me" with the Willie Webb Singers on the Philadelphia based Gotham label #671 in September, 1950 entitled, "Every Day, Every Hour". The flip side would feature Ozella Weber on "He's The One". He would later find success with his own group, The Bradford Singers.

The Alex Bradford Singers first professional recording on Apollo Records was:

#244   Now Lord - led by Willie Lee Owens
Let The Heavenly Light Shine On Me - led by Martha Rose Farrow
(Recorded in August, 1951)

Alex's biggest gospel selection, **"Too Close To Heaven"**, was published by the Roberta Martin Studio of Gospel Music and recorded by Eugene Smith and the Martin Singers in November, 1952. It was not until June, 1953 that Alex Bradford and The Bradford Specials (James Brandon, Charles E. Campbell, Louis Gibson, Billy Harper and Jonathan Jackson) recorded the selection for Specialty Records in Hollywood, California. That song, with the aiding of Roberta Martin and the Martin Singers molded Alex Bradford into a national and later, international gospel sensation.

James Cleveland, a member of the Pilgrim Baptist Church, where Thomas Dorsey was choral director began submitting several copies of his works to the Martin Studio for publishing. Cleveland, who was born and raised in Chicago; earned a great respect and gained countless musical knowledge from Roberta Martin and her step daughter,: Little Lucy Smith. "Bert" as Roberta was sometimes called, published his early career compositions. Lucy helped to teach him to play the piano. Eugene Smith and Myrtle Scott became his favorite Martin Singers. Writing such immortal pieces as: **(1) Saved, (2) Every Now and Then, (3) Grace, (4) Had It Not Been For Him, and (5) Since I Met Him** truly attest that James Cleveland was going to become a master songwriter, singer and arranger of gospel music. He would later take gospel music to a new level when he founded the Gospel Music Workshop of America (GMWA) which preserved the history and heritage of gospel music. It also spotlighted its performers; promoters; producers and enthusiasts.

In late 1950, James Cleveland moved to Philadelphia where he started his first gospel group: **The Gospelaires of Philadelphia.** He, along with two of the most popular Roberta Martin Singers: Norsalus McKissick and Bessie Folk held their first recording session for Apollo Records in October, 1950 where they recorded three selections. Two selections: *The Lifeboat is Coming and I Call Jesus My Rock*: both led by Bessie Folk; and *Every Day*, led by Norsalus McKissick. Their latter recording session, held in January, 1951; James Cleveland & The Gospelaires recorded three more selections. One of their first recordings was the Lucy Smith (Matthews) selection, *"Oh, What A Time"* along with Norslaus singing *"Talk About A Child"* and Bessie singing *"He's Pleading In Glory For Me".*

The Gospelaires were together only a short time, partly due to the fact that as Eugene stated

> *"whenever they would sing, people thought that they were another Martin Singers group as they*

*had two of their most popular members: Norsalus and Bessie. Some people even start calling them: **The Roberta Martin Specials.** There was only one Roberta Martin Singers group".*

The Gospelaires, however, gave James time enough to showcase his ability to arrange and work with a professional gospel singing group as both leader and musician. After the disbandment of the Gospelaires, Norsalus returned to the Martin Singers in 1951 and Bessie returned to the Martin Singers in 1955. James would find fame along with fellow friend, Albertina Walker in a group called **The Caravans**.

Throughout the 1950's; commonly known as the *Golden Era of Gospel Music;* Mrs. Roberta Martin and her group: the Roberta Martin Singers became the catalyst or the breeding ground for several singers to gain musical notoriety.

Another pupil of Roberta Martin to achieve that status was Robert Anderson.

Robert Anderson
Photo: courtesy Eugene Smith collection

Robert, who began with Roberta Martin in the early 1930's as a member of the Original Martin and Frye Quartet, would later find fame and gain experience of singing and traveling with the late Rev. R.L. Knowles. According to Eugene Smith, ***"Robert was converted on the 4th Sunday in July, 1935 at the Ebenezer Baptist Church and later baptized the following month"***. Robert sang with the Martin and Frye Quartet and later the Roberta Martin Singers until 1939.

In 1939, he and R.L. Knowles ventured to California to carry the new gospel music to an untouched area. By 1940, he was back in the Chicago area: and back singing with the Roberta Martin Singers as Robert was not too fond of traveling. In 1943, he substituted for Mrs. Roberta Martin at the National Baptist Convention. There, he sang the selection, "Something Within Me" and literally tore up the convention. After that, his individual career began to soar.

Later in 1943, he moved to Gary, Indiana and formed the Good Shepherd Singers and the Good Shepherd House of Music. The music publishing house stored all of his musical sheet music masterpieces and the singers: **Elyse Yancey, Gladys Scoggins, Vera Salone and Betty Jones** blended their voices together; bringing those songs to life with Robert Anderson at the piano.

In 1948, Robert Anderson became the Minister of Music for the Greater Harvest Baptist Church in Chicago and in August 1949, Robert Anderson and The Greater Harvest Choir went into the studio and recorded the first of several gospel masterpieces. In that first session in August 1949, the following recordings were produced:

My Home Over There
King Jesus Will Roll All Burdens Away
Jesus Is My Friend
Eternal Home

Then some of the personnel changed. The new version of the Good Shephard Singers featured:

Elyse Yancey
Ora Lee Hopkins – who replaced Vera Salone

Irma Gwynn – who replaced Gladys Scoggins Betty Jones.

Additional shifting and replacing voices would soon form the nucleus of a new group. Robert's new voices- consisting of **Ora Lee Hopkins, Irma Gywnn, Nellie Grace Daniels and Elyse Yancey** sang first as **Robert Anderson and His Singers.** Then in early 1951, Robert changed the name to **Robert Anderson and His Gospel Caravan** and later: with Albertina Walker replacing Irma Gwynn: **Robert Anderson and The Caravans.**

After the folding of Robert Anderson's Caravan group, he traveled extensively until 1957. He returned to Greater Harvest Baptist Church in 1957 and received a Gold plaque from radio DJ: Rev. Watley for the selection, "If Jesus Had To Pray": an Apollo recording produced in mid 1955 with Roberta Martin accompanying on the piano and Robert Wooten on the organ..

The Caravans, founded by Albertina Walker in 1952 was an offshoot of the old Robert Anderson inspired singing group. Albertina Walker's original Caravans consisted of herself, Elyse Yancey, Nellie Grace Daniels and Ora Lee Hopkins: all members of Robert Anderson's former Gospel Caravans. Their original organist was Chicago's own Louise Overall Weaver. Their original pianist, Edward Robinson was later replaced by James Cleveland: who was a musical product of Roberta Martin and "Little" Lucy Smith.

The Caravans: circa mid 1950's
Johneron Davs, Louise McDowell,
Gloria Griffin, Casietta George,
Albertina Walker, James Cleveland
Photo: courtesy Eugene Smith collection

Another member of the Martin and Frye Quartet, later the Roberta Martin Singers who became a musical icon throughout the 1950's was **Professor Willie Webb.** Webb, throughout the 1940's was the capable assistant to Roberta Martin in the music department: assisting her many times on the piano and organ.

In 1949, Willie formed his own group: **The Willie Webb Singers.** That group would produce several singers who would spiral to international gospel fame. One of their earliest big hits was the popular, *"Calling Jesus, My Rock":* popularized by the late Mrs. Sylvia Boddie and the Great

Harvest Baptist Church choir of Chicago, Ill.

Prof. Willie Webb
Photo courtesy: Chicago Public
Library – Lucy Collier collection

In September, 1950; the Willie Webb Singers ventured into the recording studio in Chicago to record a series of selections with the following personnel: ***Willie Webb, Alex Bradford, Allen W. McClinton, Ozella Weber Mosley Clifton, Oralee Thurston, Edna Coles and Elizabeth Mitchell***. Later, Webb would employ such singers as ***Imogene Green, Clifton Medley and Albertina Walker***. Webb would return to The Roberta Martin Singers to work with them throughout the mid 1950's before forming the

Willie Webb Choir: which recorded on B & F Records in early 1961.

Rev. Stanley Keeble, founder of the Gospel Heritage Museum of Chicago and a former disciple of Willie Webb shared a funny story about Willie. Stanley shared;

> *"Webb was having his annual concert. His guest were: Bro. Joe May; the Davis Sisters and The Clara Ward Singers. It had rained "cats and dogs that day". His sister, Juanita Ludlow was on the door. When we drove up to the church, he (Webb) sent me in the church to see how scarce the people were. When I went into the church, Juanita asked me, "where's Webb?" I said, "sitting in the car". Juanita went to the car and saw Webb crying. She said, "why u crying"? You better get out of this car and get inside that church – it was jammed and packed*

Three other gospel singing groups rightfully credit their inspiration to gospel singing to the Roberta Martin Singers.

In the early 1940's; Gertrude Murphy Ward and her daughters: Clara and Willa Ward would soon get a musical boost through the assistance of the Roberta Martin Singers. The Martin Singers were invited to sing at the White Rock Baptist Church in Philadelphia. In the audience at the White Rock Church were The Ward Trio: consisting of Gertrude, Clara and Willa. After hearing the Roberta Martin Singers, the Wards was spiritually moved and inspired to expand the group from a trio to a full group: thus, the concept of The (Famous) Ward Singers were born. Gertrude Murphy Ward, Clara's mother and group business manager soon employed Marion Williams from Florida, Henrietta "Madame" Waddy, Francis Steadman, Catherine "Kitty" Parham and Thelma Jackson from the Philadelphia-Baltimore region. These and countless other singers: such as Martha Bass, Ethel Gilbert and Marguerite Shaw were later employed to assist Clara as she ministered to the masses of people with her songs of Zion. Several of their songs: which included **"Jesus, Precious King" "Each Day" and "Stretch Out"** were early 1949 recordings of the Famous Clara Ward Singers and were either published and/or copyrighted by the Roberta Martin Studio of Gospel Music.

Ruth "Baby Sis", Thelma, Audrey and Alfreda Davis: known as ***The Davis Sisters*** were also from Philadelphia, Pennsylvania and was another group that received spiritual encouragement after hearing Roberta Martin and her singers.

Growing up in the Fire Baptized Holiness Church, they heard the Martin Singers during their singing revival at White Rock Baptist Church and like Clara Ward and her mother, Gertrude; were further inspired to keep on singing the gospel. They sang and recorded many classic selections for Gotham Records- located in Philadelphia, including **"We're Marching To Zion"** and **Too Close To Heaven,** and **"More Than All"** on the Savoy Recording label. All of these selections were published by the Roberta Martin Studio of Gospel Music.

Another recount from Eugene Smith was:

"We were singing in Deleware in a service with Ruth Davis and The Davis Sisters. Ruth began to sing The Old Ship of Zion and the Davis Sisters tore that church in pieces. Norsalus looked at me and said, "I hope Mrs. Martin don't play that tonight cause Baby Sis just sunk the old ship".

As pioneers of gospel music, the Roberta Martin Singers traveled all over the country carrying *"words of life on wings of a song"*.

While in Alabama, they toured Birmingham and the rest is history. As history stated, the Roberta Martin Singers: *consisting of Roberta Martin, Eugene Smith, Norsalus McKissick, Bessie Folk, Willie Webb and Robert Anderson* sang "It's A Highway To Heaven" at the 1940 National Baptist Convention and that singing rendition inspired Mildred Miller and Odessa Edwards to form a gospel singing group. These two young ladies: along with fellow Birmingham citizen Evelyn Hardy formed one of the greatest female singing groups in history: **The Original Gospel Harmonettes.**

The Original Gospel Harmonettes of Birmingham, Ala.
back to front: Willie Mae Newberry, Vera Kolb,
Mildred Miller, Odessa Edwards, Dorothy Love
photo: courtesy Eugene Smith collection

This group, consisting of Vera Kolb, Mildred Miller, Odessa Edwards, Willie Mae Newberry and Evelyn Starks recorded their first session for RCA in June, 1949: recording several songs published by Roberta Martin's Studio of Gospel Music such as **Only A Look, He's All I Need and Nothing Can Change Me.** The rich blending of this female group-with the infusion of a young Dorothy Love kept their sound vibrant for many years.

Roberta Martin Austin always had a special love for young people and children. Eugene once told me of an incident that changed Roberta's life forever.

> *"In 1949, we were singing in New York City and Roberta was to meet us in NYC and sing with us that night. That evening, right before we were to go to the service, I went down to the train station to pick up Roberta. When she arrived, I noticed that she had a little baby in her arms. I said, "Bert" we have to get to the church, whose baby do you have. She said, "my baby". I said, "girl, stop joking and take that baby to his mother so we can get to the church. Again she said, "that's my baby". Seeing she was serious, I was then introduced to Roberta Martin's baby: Master Leonard Austin: affectionately known as "Sonny"*

Roberta Martin Austin & Leonard Austin
Photo: courtesy of Leonard "Sonny" Austin

Throughout the golden era of the **1950's;**, the Roberta Martin Singers traveled across the United States of America and were the featured singers at some of the nations largest and most prestigious churches: including **Washington**

Temple COGIC- Brooklyn, New York - pastored by Bishop F.D. Washington and Mde. Ernestime Washington; **New Bethel Baptist Church-** Detroit, Michigan - pastored by Rev. C.L. Franklin and the famed **Abysinnian Baptist Church-** in New York City.

One church in particular, each year, during the Holy Week: **from Palm Sunday to Easter Sunday,** the group served as the featured singing evangelists at the **Bible Way Holiness Church** in Washington, DC, pastured by Bishop Smallwood E. Williams. It was there at the Bibleway Church, that the Roberta Martin Singers became acquainted with the pastor's daughter, **Pearl Williams-Jones**. She, along with another colleugue Dr. Bernice Reagon would spotlight the Roberta Martin Singers in the city of Washington, D.C., in future years to come. It was also there that Richard Smallwood, present day gospel icon first fell captive under the music of Roberta Martin.

Another important figure in the history of the Black Church, Detroit native Rev. Clarence LaVaughn Franklin- affectionately known as Rev. C.L. Franklin travelled all across the United States; preaching the gospel and producing such classic sermons as *"Dry Bones In The Valley", "The Eagle Stirreth The Nest" and "Ye Are The Salt of The Earth".* It was during this time, that he employed the Roberta Martin Singers to serve as the musical accompaniment to his sermonic revivals. As Eugene stated, *"we would sing and Rev. C.L. Franklin would preach".*

Rev. Clarence LaVaughn Franklin
Affectionately known as Rev. C.L. Franklin
Photo: courtesy Eugene Smith collection
national Chess Records recording artist

The Roberta Martin Singers
Circa; 1951
Left: Myrtle Scott, Delois Barrett, Bessie Folk, Willie Webb & Eugene Smith
Right: Ms. Roberta Martin on piano
(photo: courtesy the Eugene Smith collection)

Also during this period known as the "Golden Era", the Roberta Martin Singers were one of the premiere artists at Apollo Records: producing a "slew" of recordings that became musical standards for many churches including their Senior Choir, Jr. Choirs, Gospel Choruses and Men's Choir. It was during this golden era that several personnel changes would take place.

Myrtle Scott and Myrtle Jackson were both significant exponents of the Roberta Martin Gospel Singers that made history during the golden gospel era.

Myrtle Scott, a native Mississippian, came to Chicago and sang briefly with Prof. Theodore R. Frye: the mentor of Roberta Martin before joining the group. She sang and toured with the Roberta Martin Singers from 1951-1952. Her voice was not as polished as Roberta's but just as captivating. Her recordings of *Where Can I Go, The Lord Will Make A Way* and *I Wanna See Jesus* are a major part of that Roberta Martin Singers musical legacy. Of these classic renditions, she paints a vivid picture of Jesus on the selection, *"I Wanna See Jesus"* as she bellows out the verse:

> **It was here he suffered, this old world below**
> **You know he bore many crosses, when he lived here long ago; But he died and went to Glory, pleading just for me**
> **He's the same Jesus . . .. I love him, he's the one I wanna see**

Myrtle Scott
Roberta Martin Singers (1951-1952)
Photo: courtesy Eugene Smith collection

APOLLO RECORDS - January, 1951

Roberta Martin piano-Contralto, Lucy Smith-Organ, Delois Barrett- Soprano, Norsalus McKissick-Tenor, Eugene Smith--Baritone, Myrtle Scott, Alto

Where Can I Go ? - Roberta Martin/Myrtle Scott — Apollo #241
The Lord Will Make A Way - Myrtle Scott — Apollo #247
I'm Sealed - Eugene Smith — Apollo #247
You'll Understand It Better - Roberta Martin — Apollo #241
I Wanna See Jesus - Myrtle Scott — Apollo #275

Myrtle Jackson
Roberta Martin Singer (1952-1953)
Photo: courtesy Eugene Smith collection

Myrtle Jackson, an olive complexted lady with a second soprano range sang several selection with the Martin Singers. Myrtle began singing in the choir at the First Church of Deliverance, under the leadership of the late Rev. Clarence H. Cobbs prior to singing with Roberta Martin and joining the Roberta Martin Singers in 1952. Under her tutelage, Myrtle's range was perfected as she sang several selections with the group. She was also an accomplished composer and owner of her own Music publishing house: The Myrtle Jackson Studio of Music. She recorded her signature song, **"Oh Lord, Remember Me"** in February, 1949 for Coral Records in New York City.

Although the Roberta Martin Singers never recorded that selection, several of her compositions were recorded by them: including the house wrecking **"Where Can I Go"**- recorded on Apollo Records with Roberta and Myrtle Scott sharing the lead and the Easter masterpiece, **"He Didn't Mind Dying"** recorded in the finest fashion around with the Martin Gospel Singers (***Martin, Scott, McKissick, Smith, Barrett and Folk***) as her background vocals and Myrtle Jackson bellowing on lead. As the lyrics were sung, your mind went straight back to Calvary as she reminded us that:

> **The soldiers stayed by Jesus, to guard where he had died**
> **My father in heaven, was watching his own child**
> **Me made the soldiers sleep, til his work was done**
> **Christ rose from the tomb, Victory he had won**

> **Oh no he didn't mind dying and he never said a word**
> **The whole earth was dark and the Heavens, red as blood**
> **Then an angel came from Heaven and stood right by his side**
> **He said, this is my beloved son, in whom I'm satisfied . . . . . .**

After her stint with the Roberta Martin Singers, she joined forces with another Chicagoan, **R.L. Knowles** to form the **Knowles and Jackson Sextet** in the late 1950's and recorded such songs on the VJ label as *"There's Room In Heaven For Me", "A Brighter Day Ahead" and "Give In Account of Your Sins".* These songs became a part of the golden gospel era repertoire.

Although their time with the Martin Singers were short lived; both Myrtle Scott and Myrtle Jackson were great assets to the music ministry of Roberta Martin and left us a lasting legacy of anointed gospel classics.

Little Lucy Smith's grandmother, Elder Lucy Smith: pastor of the All Nations Pentecostal Church passed away on July 3, 1952. Eugene Smith described what he remembered about the funeral:

> *The funeral of Elder Lucy Smith was one of the biggest that Chicago had ever saw. People from everywhere came to pay their respects. Roberta Martin provided the piano accompaniment and*

Willie Webb served as organist. Gladys Beamon, lead singer of the Lucy Smith Singers led the choir in the stirring "In The Sweet Bye and Bye". Madame Willie Mae Ford Smith sang Oh! What A Beautiful City. The great Mahalia Jackson led the Dorsey composition "It's My Desire". Ora Lee Hopkins, a member then of the Caravans led "Get Away Jordan" and Willie Webb led the Little Lucy composition, "Oh What A Time". Norsalus, Delois, Bessie, Myrtle Scott and I all sang in the choir. I have never seen anything like it ever.

The funeral of Elder Lucy Smith (1952)
Mrs. Roberta Martin (far right) on the piano -
Mr. Willie Webb (far left) on the organ
Photo: courtesy of the Lucy Smith Collier
collection of the Chicago Public Library

Below is a discography of the recordings of the Roberta Martin Singers while on Apollo Records. Most of their recordings featured Roberta Martin on piano, Little Lucy Smith or Willie Webb on organ and singers: Roberta, Willie, Eugene, Bessie (who would return to record in 1955), Norsalus and Delois along with a smidgeon of Myrtle Scott and Myrtle Jackson.

APOLLO RECORDS - May, 1952
Roberta Martin piano-Contralto, Lucy Smith-Organ, Delois Barrett- Soprano, Norsalus McKissick-Tenor, Eugene Smith--Baritone, Myrtle Scott, Alto, Myrtle Jackson, Soprano

Oh Lord, Stand By Me - Eugene Smith	Apollo #270
Come In The Room - Eugene Smith	Apollo #261
He's My Light - Norsalus McKissick	Apollo #261
He Didn't Mind Dying - Myrtle Jackson	Apollo #270

APOLLO RECORDS - November, 1952
Roberta Martin piano-Contralto, Willie Webb-Organ, Delois Barrett- Soprano, Norsalus McKissick-Tenor, Eugene Smith--Baritone, Myrtle Scott- Alto, Myrtle Jackson, Soprano

After It's All Over - Eugene Smith/Roberta Martin	Apollo #272
I'm Too Close - Eugene Smith	Apollo #279
The Old Account - Norsalus McKissick	Apollo #272
Let God Abide - Eugene Smith	Apollo #275
I'm Determined - Eugene Smith/Norsalus McKissick	Apollo #487

APOLLO RECORDS - January, 1953

Roberta Martin piano-Contralto, Willie Webb-Organ, Delois Barrett- Soprano, Norsalus McKissick-Tenor, Eugene Smith- Baritone, Little Lucy Smith- Soprano

Since I Met Jesus - Norsalus McKissick	Apollo #281
Oh, Say So - Delois Barrett	Apollo #292
Keep On Trusting- Eugene Smith	Apollo #281
Is There Anybody Here - Eugene Smith	Apollo #297
I'm Gonna Praise His Name - Roberta Martin	Apollo #292
Marching To Zion - Eugene Smith	Apollo #279

APOLLO RECORDS - early, 1954

Roberta Martin piano-Contralto, Willie Webb-Organ, Delois Barrett- Soprano, Norsalus McKissick-Tenor, Eugene Smith- Baritone, Little Lucy Smith- Soprano

I'm Just Waiting On the Lord - Norsalus McKissick	Apollo #285
I've Got A Home For You - Norsalus McKisick	Apollo #297
Shine Heavenly Light - Eugene Smith	Apollo #285

APOLLO RECORDS - mid 1955

Roberta Martin piano-Contralto, Willie Webb-Organ, Delois Barrett- Soprano, Norsalus McKissick-Tenor, Eugene Smith- Baritone, Bessie Folk, Alto

He's Using Me - Eugene Smith/Norsalus McKissick	Apollo #299

Trouble In My Way - Norsalus McKissick   Apollo #305
I'll Do What You Want Me To Do - Bessie Folk   Apollo #301
Come Into My Heart Lord Jesus - Delois Barrett   Apollo #301
I'm Saved - Eugene Smith   Apollo #299
There's A Man - Eugene Smith   Apollo #305

APOLLO RECORDS - From Unknown session
Roberta Martin piano-Contralto, Willie Webb-Organ, Delois Barrett- Soprano, Norsalus McKissick-Tenor, Eugene Smith- Baritone, **possibly**: Myrtle Scott-Alto, Myrtle Jackson-Soprano

> I Don't Mind - led by Norsalus McKissick
> He's Always Right There - led by Eugene Smith
> Do You Know Jesus ? - led by Eugene Smith

Although becoming Savoy Recording artists in 1956, Bess Berman's Apollo Records released several LP albums of the Roberta Martin Singers: composed of many of their familiar recordings including......

Here This Sunday
The Original Roberta Martin Singers
Apollo LP 480

* the first Gold Record for the Martin Singers is released on this album with The Old Ship of Zion

Where Can I Go? - Myrtle Scott
Oh Say So - Delois Barrett
We're Marchin To Zion - Eugene Smith
What A Blessing - Delois Barrett
I Don't Mind - Norsalus McKissick
He Didn't Mind Dying - Myrtle Jackson

Let It Be - Delois Barrett
I'm Sealed - Eugene Smith
What A Friend - Roberta Martin
By and By - Roberta Martin
Old Ship of Zion - Norsalus McKissick
Satisfied - Eugene Smith

Prayer Meeting
The Roberta Martin Singers
Apollo LP 487

* The second recorded Gold Record is recorded here with Only A Look

Do You Know Him - Eugene Smith

I'm Gonna Praise His Name - Roberta Martin
Come Into My Heart - Delois Barrett
I'm Saved - Eugene Smith
He's Always Right There - Eugene Smith
I'll Do What You Want Me To Do - Bess Folk
There's A Man - Eugene Smith
After It's All Over - Roberta Martin
Only A Look - Bess Folk
Is There Anybody Here - Eugene Smith
I'm Determined - Eugene Smith
I'm Just Waiting On The Lord - Norsalus McKissick

Mahalia with the Greatest Spiritual Singers
Apollo LP 489

Come In The Room - The Roberta Martin Singers - led by Eugene Smith
He's Using Me - The Roberta Martin Singers - led by Norsalus McKissick and Eugene Smith
Since I Met Jesus - The Roberta Martin Singers - led by Norsalus McKissick
Do You Know Jesus - The Roberta Martin Singers - led by Eugene Smith

The Old Ship of Zion
The Roberta Martin Singers
Apollo/Kenwood LP 507

The Old Ship of Zion - Norsalus McKissick
What A Friend - Roberta Martin
Come In The Room - Eugene Smith

Too Close To Heaven - Eugene Smith
Only A Look - Bess Folk
Come Into My Heart - Delois Barrett
I'm Gonna Praise His Name - Roberta Martin
Since I Met Jesus - Norsalus McKissick
What A Blessing - Delois Barrett
I'm Saved - Eugene Smith
He's Using Me - Norsalus McKissick/Eugene Smith
He's My Light - Norsalus McKissick
I'll Do What You Want Me To Do - Bess Folk
The Old Account - Norsalus McKissick

While recording gospel masterpieces and traveling all over the United States of America, the Roberta Martin Singers were in service, many times, singing in the absence of their leader: Mrs. Roberta Martin Austin. Since turning over the groups management to Eugene Smith in 1949, Mrs. Martin had become more focused on the success of the publishing house: in addition to performing her role as wife to Mr. James "Jimmy" Austin and mother to her son, Leonard "Sonny" Austin.

Leonard "Sonny" Austin, Roberta Martin Austin and unidentified man
Photo: courtesy of Leonard Austin collection

4901 Woodlawn Ave.
the latter years home of James Austin
& Roberta Martin Austin
This is the home Roberta Martin was residing when
she became ill and ultimately passed away
Photo: courtesy of Joseph Middleton – Houston, Texas

As "Sonny" Austin: Mrs. Martin's son so lovingly remembered, ***"At 4901 Woodlawn, you did not play or even venture into the living room without her permission. Mother did not play"*** . . .

Between the time that Roberta Martin left Ebenezer Baptist Church and prior to coming to Mt. Pisgah, she served as Directress at the Shiloh Baptist Church ; pastored by the late Rev. L.W. Hall: which was Roberta's brother in law. It was there that she met Leona Price who would-in later years- serve as her personal secretary and business manager of the Martin Music Studio. At Shiloh, Roberta instituted the fourth Sunday night musicals-where Chicago's best came to sing.

Roberta also served as Minister of Music throughout the 1950's at the South Park Baptist Church – pastured by Rev. E.R. Williams. It was at South Park, that Roberta Martin's musical expertise was further enhanced and showcased as the South Park Church held its weekly Sunday broadcast over WGES-AM in Chicago and multiplied thousands and maybe millions were blessed to hear her sing, play and arrange.

In January of **1956**; the Roberta Martin Singers were one of the featured guest artists at the homegoing service of Thelma Davis Blassingame: one of the original members of The Davis Sisters of Philadelphia.

In that same year; Roberta Martin began a musical merger with the Mt. Pisgah Baptist Church which would last for twelve years. It was in that year that she became the Minister of Music for the Mt. Pisgah Church, under the pastorate of Dr. Joseph Wells. She then served as Minister of Music until 1968.

Roberta Martin, directing the choirs at the Mt. Pisgah Baptist Church in Chicago
Photo: courtesy of Leonard Austin collection

Mrs. Roberta Martin & The Mt. Pisgah Choir
Photo: courtesy Leonard Austin collection

In 1956; Willie Webb resigned his position as musician for the Roberta Martin Singers: having served in the position as organist and musical assistant to Roberta Martin from 1933 to 1949 and from 1953-1956. He was replaced permanently by "Little" Lucy Smith in 1956 as organist. She would also become a featured background vocal, anointed soloist and permanent assistant musical to Mrs. Martin.

In **1957**, the Roberta Martin Singers added a new singing sensation to their roster of established lyricists. They also changed recording labels: moving from the Apollo Recording company to a new venue- Savoy Records.

Gloria Griffin was a former background singer with the Clara Ward Singers and the Caravans. She would soon gain national and international gospel stardom as a member of the Martin Singers. Gloria always said that she was a product of Eugene Smith.

Gloria Griffin

Gloria got her initial formal musical training while singing in the Radio Choir of the Greater Harvest Baptist Church: pastured by the late Rev. Lewis Boddie. Gloria was approached by Eugene Smith one Sunday night and was asked to become a Martin Singer. He wanted her telephone number and she graciously gave it to him.

Gloria was at that time: traveling, singing and gaining experience as a gospel singer with Prophet Jones of St. Louis, Mo. It was during this time that another Martin Singer, Bessie Folk, encountered a near fatal automobile accident and Mrs. Martin sent her a telegram wanting Gloria to come home and rehearse to go with the group on the next road trip.

Although sometimes unsure of her ability to sing in a group of the magnitude of the Martin Singers, Gloria persisted to give it her all. Mrs. Martin pushed her with praise, spirit and encouragement and she, Delois and Lucy became as gospel singing triplets. Delois Barrett Campbell stated that "Gloria was a true killer when it came to singing a song" Her introduction to the gospel music world with the Roberta Martin Singers came with the song: an old traditional spiritual-arranged by Roberta Martin entitled, **"Nobody Knows the Troubles I've Seen"**.

The same year and time, **Savoy Record Executives**: Herman Lubinsky and Ozzie Cadera signed the Roberta Martin Singers to an exclusive contract. After a successful run at Apollo Records, Mrs. Martin took her singers into the New York studios and the result was the first of several album releases on Savoy Records.

Mrs. Martin: being a godly woman was also a firm-yet compassionate businesswoman. She knew how to negotiate a contract. The late Rev. Lawrence Roberts, former pastor of the First Baptist Church in Nutley, New Jersey and a liaison between many African American gospel artists and Savoy Records once told of an incident between Savoy Execs and Mrs. Martin. Lawrence said,

> *"Mrs. Martin would come into Herman Lubinsky's office. Say a few words, flash her smile and then Mr. Lubinsky would get out his checkbook. After leaving his office, he (Lubinsky) would say, "Roberts" how much did I pay to her. Lubinsky referred to Mrs. Martin as the HELEN HAYES of Gospel Music."*

The first album recorded and released for the Roberta Martin Singers on the Savoy label was entitled:

Twelve Inspirational Songs
The Roberta Martin Singers - Savoy 14008
Recorded, 1957
* the first Roberta Martin Singers
album on Savoy Records
* Romance Watson and Gloria Griffin
first heard as lead on this album

The Roberta Martin Singers (late 1950's)
Photo: courtesy of Eugene Smith collection

This album was a result of two successful recording sessions at the Savoy Recording studios in New York City.

SAVOY RECORDS - January 31, 1957
Roberta Martin piano-Contralto, Little Lucy Smith-Organ, Delois Barrett- Soprano, Norsalus McKissick-Tenor, Eugene Smith- Baritone, Gloria Griffin- Alto, Romance Watson

>Walk In Jerusalem - Eugene Smith
>Nothing But A God - Norsalus McKissick
>Every Now and Then - Eugene Smith
>When He Sets Me Free - Romance Watson
>Only A Look - Delois Barrett Campbell
>God Is So Good To Me - Romance Watson/ Norsalus McKissick

SAVOY RECORDS - April 12, 1957
Roberta Martin piano-Contralto, Little Lucy Smith-Organ, Delois Barrett- Soprano, Norsalus McKissick-Tenor, Eugene Smith- Baritone, Gloria Griffin- Alto, Romance Watson

>Nobody Knows - Gloria Griffin
>Teach Me Lord To Wait - Delois Barrett
>The Crucifixion - Eugene Smith
>It's Amazing - Norsalus McKissick
>Sinner Man - Roberta Martin
>In These Dark Hours of Distress - Eugene Smith & Lucy Smith

***In These Dark Hours of Distress** is the first recorded selection where Little Lucy Smith takes a definitive role as soloist. This song is also a remake of the early 40's repertoire selection: **Stretch Out**

In January, **1958**; Roberta Martin and her singers recorded possibly the biggest selling song in their musical career. The leader of the song ***GRACE*** was a seasoned Norsalus McKissick and its writer was James Cleveland.. As Eugene once stated:

"We were singing in Baltimore when McKissick began to sing Grace. When he finished singing the song, none of the Martin Singers were left standing and the paramedics literally had to be called in"

Other than "Grace"; that recording session in January also produced several other notable selections including:

Certainly Lord - Gloria Griffin
Talk About A Child - Romance Watson
I Can Make It - Eugene Smith
Ride On, King Jesus - Roberta Martin
He'll Make You Happy - Delois Barrett

Sonny Austin stated that, *"of all the songs that I saw mom sang, I felt that Ride On, King Jesus was probably her most anointed message".*

On July 6, 1958; the Roberta Martin Singers were the special guest of the Famous Ward Singers at their 25th Anniversary in Philadelphia. At the anniversary, they introduced an unrecorded song "God Specializes" to the audience and the result was maddening. As Gene put it, **"lawd, Mrs. Ward screamed and shouted so after Gloria sang, 'til I know they heard her in Baltimore".**

Later in that same month, the Roberta Martin Singers once again ventured into the recording studios of Savoy Records and once again, a series of recordings were produced. One selection would be as big as GRACE if not bigger. In that recording session, Gloria Griffin asked a question:

> **Have you any river, that seems uncross able**
> **Have you any mountains that you can't tunnel through**
> **GOD SPECIALIZES, in things thought impossible**
> **And he will do, what no other power, Holy Ghost power, can do . . . .**

The song, **GOD SPECIALIZES** gave hope to multiplied thousands of believers as they would speak to any condition and/or situation and declare that *"he will do, what no other power, can do".*

GOD SPECIALIZES

AS SUNG AND RECORDED BY
THE ROBERTA MARTIN SINGERS

WORDS AND MUSIC
by
GLORIA GRIFFIN

ARRANGED BY
ROBERTA MARTIN

PRICE 35¢

PUBLISHED BY
THE ROBERTA MARTIN STUDIO OF MUSIC
1308 E. 47th Street, Chicago 15, Ill.

MADE IN U.S.A.

Used by permission from Leonard Austin

Grace was written by upcoming gospel giant, James Cleveland: who was not yet a minister and God Specializes was written by Gloria Griffin. These two selections were part of the album, released by Savoy Records entitled:

"GRACE"
The Roberta Martin Singers - Savoy 14022
Recorded, 1958
* possibly the most famous Martin Singers album
* two Roberta Martin Singers Gold
Records are featured on this album:
Grace and God Specializes

Other selections recorded at that July 23, 1958 session for Savoy Records were as follows:

I Found Him - Norsalus McKissick
Rock My Soul - Romance Watson
He's Already Done What He Said He'd Do - Roberta Martin
Back To The Fold - Delores Barrett Campbell

The success of the album GRACE: along with the smashing success of the two singles: **GRACE and GOD SPECIALIZES** afforded the Roberta Martin Singers not one, but two Gold Records from the Savoy Recording Company.

During their tenure with Apollo Records, the Roberta Martin Singers received two Gold Records for the recordings: **Only A Look** - the theme song of the Roberta

Martin Singers for many years and for **The Old Ship of Zion**. Now on Savoy Records, they would receive the same accolades for the selections: **Grace** and **God Specializes.**

"As a note of trivia: Norsalus McKissick was perfoming the lead on two of their early gold Records: The Old Ship Of Zion (1949) and Grace. (1958)"

As a child, Archie Dennis grew up listening to the Roberta Martin Singers and as a young man, saw them one evening at the Bibleway Holiness Church in Washington, DC. He later became a member of the Maceo Woods Singers in Chicago. While in Chicago, Rev. Kyles took him to a service at the Liberty Baptist Church where he was asked to sing. Ironically, the lady playing the piano was the incomparable: Roberta Martin. She was impressed with his voice texture and vocal quality, but there was no vacancy in the group at the time. But God's plan was divinely being worked out. About a year and a half later, Archie was called, by Eugene Smith- at the urging of Mrs. Martin and asked to join the group. That was in **1958**.

Rev. Archie Dennis, Jr.

Archie began to rehearse with the group and ventured on his first trip with the Roberta Martin Singers to Houston, Texas with the Rev. C.L. Franklin of Detroit, Michigan. They performed at the famed Music Hall. As Eugene stated:

"The service started each night at 7:00 P.M. If you did not get there by 5 o'clock, there was no room. People packed that place every night"

Although Lucy had taken over a large percentage of the musical accompaniment as Roberta Martin was spending an enormous amount of time with the publishing house; beginning in **1959**, "Little" Lucy Smith would occasionally accompany the group on the piano on the studio recordings- leaving the duties of organist many times to the Savoy studio musicians.

In April, the Roberta Martin Singers ventured back into the studios of Savoy Records to record their next million selling section, **"God Is Still On The Throne"**. This and nine other selections, recorded on April 17th and 23rd would ultimately give the Roberta Martin Singers their next Gold Record: for the title selection.

"GOD IS STILL ON THE THRONE"

The Roberta Martin Singers - Savoy 14031
Recorded, 1959

* first recorded performance of Archie Dennis, Jr.

Savoy Records: April 17, 1959
Personnel: Roberta Martin, Little Lucy Smith, Delois Barrett, Gloria Griffin, Norsalus Mckissick, Eugene Smith, Archie Dennis- who replaces Romance Watson

> He's So Divine - Delois Barrett Campbell
> He's All I Need - Norsalus McKissick
> Step In Jesus - Archie Dennis
> God Is Still On The Throne - Gloria Griffin
> That Great Judgment Day - Eugene Smith/Roberta Martin/Delois Barrett
> He Laid His Hands On Me - Eugene Smith

Savoy Records: April 23, 1959
Personnel: Roberta Martin, Little Lucy Smith, Delois Barrett, Gloria Griffin, Norsalus Mckissick, Eugene Smith, Archie Dennis- who replaces Romance Watson

> Hold Me Jesus - Norsalus McKissick
> Hold The Light - Gloria Griffin & Little Lucy Smith
> Jesus Will Hear You Pray - Delois Barrett
> Since He Lightened My Heavy Load - Eugene Smith

Later, the Roberta Martin Singers were the featured guest at the **1959 "World's Greatest Gospel Caravan"** at the Shrine Auditorium in Los Angeles, California. They were also the special musical guests at the National Baptist Convention at the invitation of Dr. J. Robert Bradley and the Church Of God In Christ convocation at the invitation of both Bishop C.H. Mason and Mother Lillian Coffey. They were also in great demand at various AME, CME and AME Zion Methodist churches throughout rural and urban areas across the nation.

The Roberta Martin Singers singing in New York City
Eugene Smith, Archie Dennis, Delois Barrett
Campbell, Roberta Martin & Gloria Griffin
Photo: courtesy Eugene Smith collection

The following is a partial list of some of the activities that Mrs. Roberta Martin Austin and the Roberta Martin Singers were involved in during the mid 1950's:

1951 (February) - The Roberta Martin Singers were presented by the Usher Board #1 of the St. Stephens Baptist Church in Kansas City

(August) – The Roberta Martin Singers sang at Washington Park in Chicago in an All Star Gospel Extravaganza which featured several top gospel singers

1953 Mrs. Roberta Martin Austin served as Mistress of Ceremonies at the Hammond Organ Scholarship program at Pilgrim Baptist Church in Chicago. Contestants included John W. Burns, Jr., Joseph Martin and Maceo Woods.

1954 (September) - The Roberta Martin Singers sang to tremendous crowds nightly at the First Baptist Church - Park and Lincoln Ave. in Cincinnati.

1956 (April) - The Roberta Martin Singers were highlighted at a program at the Carter Temple CME Church: Rev. S.J. Laws, Pastor

(October) - Mrs. Roberta Martin Austin spearheaded the "On To Victory" Dinner: sponsored by the Mt. Pisgah Bapt. Church as part of the Building Fund campaign

1957 (October) - Gospel Singer Robert Anderson served as special guest soloist at the 24th anniversary program for The Roberta Martin Singers at the Tabernacle Baptist Church: 4130 S. Indiana

(November) - The Roberta Martin Singers rendered service at the Bibleway Church of the Air at an appreciation musical for Edna Tubbs of Cosmetics Renown Reveals.

1958 (June) - The Roberta Martin Singers appear at the Cottage Grove Baptist Church in Chicago in a "Grand Homecoming" musical

(July) - The Roberta Martin Singers receive rave reviews on the "Pet" Sunday Morning Radio Show on WBEE. Sid McCoy served as MC

(December) - The Roberta Martin Singers appear at a Gospel Spectacular at the Tabernacle Baptist Church along with Gospel Clefs of New Jersey, the Sallie Martin Singers, Rev. Cleophus Robinson and Rev. James Cleveland & The Gospel Chimes. "Singing Sammy Lewis" served as coordinator.

1959 (May) - The Roberta Martin Singers join Mahalia Jackson at Madison Square Gardens in New York City.

(July) - The Roberta Martin Singers appear at a Summer Music Festival at the Divine Healing Temple in Chicago. The Martin Singers had just returned from an extensive singing tour.

In late 1959, Archie Dennis, the newest member of the Roberta Martin was inducted into the military. During that time, Eugene Smith had recruited **Mr. Stanley Harold Johnson** from Baltimore, Maryland to fill in for Archie. Harold had a baritone voice similar to that of Archie's and Romance, but his singing style was totally different from that of both Archie or Romance. Harold would travel and sing with the Martin Singers until Archie would return from his military stint. Harold would later come into his own with the assistance of a 1961 recording.

The 1960's

The Roberta Martin Singers
"The dean of Gospel Singers"

Harold Johnson, Roberta Martin, Gloria Griffin, Norsalus McKissick, "Little" Lucy Smith and Eugene Smith
Photo: courtesy Eugene Smith collection

The era of the **1960's** brought an even greater spiritual charge to the Roberta Martin Singers. After having celebrated over 25 years of singing the gospel and over 20 years of publishing and distributing sheet music and music books all over the country, the Martin Singers were still climbing the ladder of evangelistic success and setting new standards and boundaries as recording artists.

The year of **1960** saw the singers go back into the Savoy recording studio in New York City and the result once again was a smash record setting session and album. Originally written and published in 1943, the selection **"Try Jesus, He Satisfies"** was rearranged from its original 1943 arrangement by the masterful collaboration of Roberta Martin and Little Lucy Smith. The result was a beautiful rendition of the song, complete with background arrangement and musical layout.

"TRY JESUS"
The Roberta Martin Singers - Savoy 14039
Recorded: 1960
* Sara McKissick, a former member of the Lucy Smith Singers is singing background on this album

The album, recorded on the Savoy label, featured the Roberta Martin regulars: ***Eugene Smith, Norsalus Mckissick, Gloria Griffin, Little Lucy Smith and Roberta Martin.***

On this album, however, Roberta brought along Mrs. Sarah McKissick: a singer from the old Lucy Smith Singers of the late 1940's to sing the soprano part. Sarah McKissick joined Roberta and Lucy as an introductory trio on the song:

Keep on praying, keep on praying
And Heaven's doors wil unlock . . . .

Then Norsalus: Sarah's former husband, belted out the lead:

"he can heal – a wounded soul – if you pray
he can make-a sinner whole- if you pray"

Singing on the Savoy album were the following selections including:

SAVOY RECORDS: January 26 - 27, 1960
PERSONNEL: Roberta Martin, Little Lucy Smith, Norsalus McKissick, Eugene Smith, Gloria Griffin, Sarah McKissick and Harold Johnson

> Try Jesus, He Satisfies - Roberta Martin
> Oh How Much He Cares - Gloria Griffin
> If You Pray - Norsalus McKissick -Trio: Roberta Martin, Lucy Smith & Sarah McKissick
> He Never Said A Word - Gloria Griffin
> It's Gonna Rain - Eugene Smith
> He Comes To See About Me - Eugene Smith
> When He Died - Roberta Martin
> Let's Go Home - Gloria Griffin
> I Need You, Lord - Norsalus McKissick

He's Leading Me - Eugene Smith

Martin Trivia: The album, "Try Jesus", is the first Roberta Martin Singers album where Delois Barrett Campbell is not a part of the vocals.

In March 1960; The Roberta Martin Singers appeared with Mrs. Lorenza Brown Porter and The Argo Singers in a benefit musical at the Olivet Baptist Church -3101 S. Parkway. The Rev. J.H. Jackson, pastor.

Later, in the month of July, Mrs. Roberta Martin Austin appeared as a solo singer- with musical associates: Prof. Thomas Dorsey, Sallie Martin, Willie Webb and Prof. Theodore Frye at the 27th anniversary for Robert Anderson: one of her early pupils at the Greater Salem Baptist Church: 215 E. 71$^{st.}$

At the 1960 National Baptist Convention in Chicago, Mrs. Martin directed the 1000 voice choir with the rendition of **GRACE:** which was written by James Cleveland; arranged by Roberta Martin and led masterfully, spiritually and prayerfully by Delois Barrett Campbell. That event was probably the highlight of 1960 for Mrs. Roberta Martin.

**Two great gospel pioneers:
Mrs. Roberta Martin and Prof. Thomas A. Dorsey**
Photo: courtesy of Leonard Austin collection

When the Roberta Martin Singers went into the Savoy Studios in **1961**; Mrs. Martin had a whole new repertoire of songs to introduce to the nation: including the selection that would be spotlighted by Harold Johnson: the singer that temporarily replaced Archie Dennis: ***"Oh, What A Day"***. As Harold would belt out the song, one could visually get a glimpse of glory.

I am waiting and watching - for that great day
Where my trials, I cannot endure
Where my sins, and sorrows are all washed away
There's be peace, and contentment, I'm sure
Where my Jesus, is awaiting me - A crown he has, you'll see
And for that day, so glad I'll be, oh what a day . . . . .

When the session had ended, the album, **"Since I Met Him"** was born. The title selection and the following selections were a part of that latest Savoy project:

"SINCE I MET HIM"
The Roberta Martin Singers - Savoy 14043
Recorded: 1961

* Only album where Harold Johnson is vocally leading a song

* ***"Only God"*** was the first selection where Little Lucy takes a complete lead alone

The first Roberta Martin Singers album where selections were recorded, but not issued. . . . . . .

February 2, 1961 - Savoy Records - New York City
Personnel: Roberta Martin, Little Lucy Smith, Norsalus McKissick, Eugene Smith, Gloria Griffin, Harold Johnson and Delois Barrett

Since I Met Him - Norsalus McKissick
Had It Not Been For Him - Gloria Griffin
Only God - Lucy Smith

I Couldn't Hear Nobody Pray - Eugene Smith
I'm His Child - Gloria Griffin
February 3, 1961 - Savoy Records - New York City

Personnel: Roberta Martin, Little Lucy Smith, Norsalus McKissick, Eugene Smith, Gloria Griffin, Harold Johnson and Delois Barrett

Cast Your Cares On Him - Roberta Martin
Beyond The Dark Clouds - Norsalus McKissick
I'll Keep On Holding, To His Hand - Gloria Griffin
All Things Are Possible - Eugene Smith
Oh, What A Day - Harold Johnson
He's Done Something For Me - Unissued
It Was The Blood - Unissued

In September 1961; Mrs. Roberta Martin Austin won the Mary Hamilton Kendrick Memorial Award of the National Gospel Symposium Association in Washington, D.C. In that same month; Mrs. Roberta Martin Austin and The Roberta Martin Singers were the featured guest for the Beautification Club of the Fellowship Baptist Church - Rev. Clay Evans, Pastor

As if her schedule as a gospel singer, songwriter, arranger and entrepreneur wasn't enough, Mrs. Roberta Martin Austin showcased her talents and knowledge of the Bible by serving as Women's Day speaker at the Mt. Pisgah Bapt. Church at 467 E. Bowen Ave in the month of October of 1961.

The holiday season saw The Roberta Martin Singers as special guests at a special Holiday Benefit and Gospel Song Festival at the DuSable High School in Chicago. Rev. E. Suddoth was the sponsor and Hammond Organ extraordinaire Mrs. Louise Overall Weaver served as chairperson

In **1962**, Roberta Martin took her troupe of singers into the Herman Lubinsky Savoy Recording Studios to put together the **"It Was The Blood"** album.

For the first time, in several years; the Roberta Martin Singers were together in the recording studio: producing a sound that was similar to that of the old Apollo Recording days: much due to the fact that Bessie Folk was back with the group for a stint. Also during that same timespan, Archie Dennis had returned to the Roberta Martin Singers from serving his country in the military.

Although the Roberta Martin Singers had never produced a Christmas album, their next project for the Savoy Recording company carried a theme of the Easter season. Although minus one of their mainstays: Norsalus McKissick from that session, the Roberta Martin Singers pumped out a series of selections including the selections **"Look Up and Live"** with duets Eugene and Bessie and **"I Shall Know Him"** with duets Roberta and Bessie where their voices blended together: reminiscent of the days of the old Apollo Recordings. Although "Old Man" McKissick was absent, the remaining voices: Delois Barrett Campbell,

Gloria Griffin and Little Lucy Smith assisted Roberta, Eugene Smith and Bessie Folk create a polished sound: deserving of music's highest honors.

"IT WAS THE BLOOD"
The Roberta Martin Singers - Savoy 14054
Recorded: 1962

"The Roberta Martin Singers salute to Easter"

SAVOY RECORDS - February 1, 1962
PERSONNEL: Roberta Martin, Little Lucy Smith, Eugene Smith, Archie Dennis, Gloria Griffin, Bessie Folk and Delois Barrett Campbell

> It Was The Blood - Eugene Smith
> Walk On By Faith - Gloria Griffin
> You've Been Truly Blessed - Archie Dennis
> Is It Nothing To You - Gloria Griffin
> Look Up And Live - Eugene Smith, Roberta Martin & Bessie Folk

SAVOY RECORDS - February 2, 1962
PERSONNEL: Roberta Martin, Little Lucy Smith, Eugene Smith, Archie Dennis, Gloria Griffin, Bessie Folk, Delois Barrett Campbell

> I Hear God - Delois Barrett Campbell
> Out Of The Depths: The Martin Ladies
> No Other Help I Know - Gloria Griffin & Roberta Martin
> I Shall Know Him - Roberta Martin & Bessie Folk

The Least That I Can Do - Gloria Griffin
He Included Me – Unissued

He Brought Me Out - Archie Dennis - issued as Savoy single #4181 was a part of that recording session, but not a release on the album.

Within that same week, on **February 8, 1962**; Little Lucy Smith recorded a series of musical selections on the Hammond Organ: including the following:

Yes, Jesus Loves Me
When The Saints Go Marching In - unissued
Just To Behold His Face
What A Friend We Have In Jesus
Everytime I Feel The Spirit
God Be With You
What A Blessing In Jesus I've Found
Jesus Lover Of My Soul
He Knows Just How Much We Can Bear
He'll Understand And Say Well Done
God Will Take Care Of You
Amazing Grace - Unissued
On The Battlefield - Unissued

The recording executives of Savoy Records marketed the album as:

"Little Lucy At The Organ"
Savoy #14056

On June 15, 1962; The Roberta Martin Singers were the featured guest at the New Testament Baptist Church on S. Normal Blvd. for the Usher's department.

The month of July, '62 was an extremely busy one for the Roberta Martin Singers and also for Mrs. Roberta Martin Austin. Mrs. Roberta Martin Austin served as guest speaker at the Divine Healing Temple for the Women's Day Service at 4800 S. Cottage Grove. Mrs. Leona Price, Mrs. Martin's personal Secretary and Business Manager of the Publishing House was the chairperson and Rev. Ella Price was the pastor.

That same time span, The Roberta Martin Singers sang at a benefit service: sponsored by gospel singing great: Mahalia Jackson to assist in the paying off of the mortgage of the South Shore Baptist Church. They were also the featured guest at the 29th Anniversary for Prof. Robert Anderson at the Hyde Park Baptist Church.

During the month of November, Eugene Smith: Business Manager and singer of the Roberta Martin Singers served as guest soloist for the Men's Day program at the Mt. Pisgah Baptist Church - of which Roberta Martin was Minister of Music.

In December, Mrs. Roberta Martin Austin's holiday gift to the city of Chicago was a Pre Yuletide Concert at the Mt. Pisgah Baptist Church - which featured a 150 voice Mass choir and guest soloist: the great, Mahalia Jackson.

Eugene Smith told me of a conversation that he and Roberta had sometime in 1962 concerning a live recording. Eugene told "Bert":

"Bert, wouldn't it be good if we could record an album right in church- That way, the people would get to hear exactly what we experience every night. Bert said, "That sounds really good". Let's see what we can do with this".

After conversing with Rev Lawrence Roberts, liasion between Savoy Records and the gospel community about the idea, it was thought that a "live" recording would be another "HIGH" in the career of The Roberta Martin Singers. After some collaboration between Roberta Martin and her singers and between Roberta Martin and the executives of Savoy Records, the project

"IN SERVICE with The Roberta Martin Singers" took shape.

"FROM OUT OF NOWHERE"
The Roberta Martin Singers - Savoy 14066
Recorded: March 6, 1963
"The only live recording of The Roberta Martin Singers"

On this project, recorded in **1963**, one would have the opportunity of hearing Eugene Smith masterfully introduce each and every selection: a technique that he introduced in the early 1940's and perfected over the years. That technique is still used by gospel singers today. Also on this recording, one would hear each and every Martin Singers as they professionally, yet spiritually interpreted each song.

As one entered the jammed, crammed and packed First Baptist Church of Nutley, New Jersey; the atmosphere was primed and ripe for gospel singing at its best. As the Roberta Martin Singers took their places: Roberta Martin and Lucy interchanged at the piano, Little Lucy Smith at the organ, Eugene Smith at the narration microphone and the singers: Delois Barrett Campbell- Soprano; Norsalus McKissick- Tenor; Gloria Griffin- Alto and Archie Dennis- Baritone at their mics; the spiritual ecstasy was about to begin.

Eugene opened up by saying,

*"One day, when I was walking in sin, with no thought of my soul. I never thought about God and his goodness to me a sinner. But my mother's prayers followed me and one day, **FROM OUT OF NOWHERE;** I found him. And oh I'm so glad, that I did."*

As Gene completed his introduction, Roberta Martin set the tone with the singing of the signature tune, "From Out of Nowhere". At the end of that selection, the remainder of the service was destined to go soaring through the clouds.

The rest of the project repertoirare: including some of the narration excerpts are as follows:

They tell me that there are 12 gates to the city, called Heaven. 3 gates in the East, 3 gates in the West, 3 gates in the North and 3 gates in the South that we may enter in. But before we reach those pearly gates, we must pass through The Gateway of Life. **The Gateway to Life is Christ.** *Led by Archie Dennis, Jr.*

Sometimes along life's journey, we find that the things we want, cost more than we can pay. But if we consider the things we cannot pay for: like the air we breathe or the water we drink. The salvation in our soul the love of God in our heart. We will then realize that the **Best Things In Life Are Free.** *Led by Delois Barrett Campbell*

Our lives are sometimes filled with storm clouds and we can find no rest, until we pray to our heavenly father: and hear him say, "Peace Be Still". Then we can feel **The Storm Is Passing Over**, *because we have the peace, deep down, in our soul. Led by Norsalus McKissick*

There is one in whom you can depend. One who never fails. And if you want a sure friend, Try God. **For There Is No Failure In God.** *Led by Norsalus McKissick*

Tell me what would you do? Tell me what would you do? Tell me **What Would You Do Without Jesus**? *Led by Archie Dennis, Jr.*

How much do I need the Lord? How long will I need him? And why do I need him? There are reasons to many to mention. But there's one thing I do know, more than all, **I Need The Lord.** *Led by Gloria Griffin*

When the light grows dim on my pathway. And it seems I'm stumbling along. When I must walk through the valley of the shadow of Death. I have but one clear call to make and that is **"Come Lord Jesus"** *and walk with me. Led by Eugene Smith*

When I come to the end of my journey and I need a helping hand. When mother, father, sister, and brother are all gone, **I Can Call Jesus, Anytime***. Led by Norsalus McKissick*

However, possibly the most soul stirring selection of the night was the dynamite selection: **"Im So Grateful"** - sung by the dynamic duo of Gloria Griffin and Little Lucy Smith. Eugene set the stage by introducing the following:

"One day Jesus met 10 lepers and healed all of them. For he is able, even to heal the lepers. 9 of them went away and never came back, but one of them came back to say, Lord, I want to thank you. I can remember the day, I remember it well when he healed me of something worse than the leprosy, he healed my sinsick soul and today-I'm returning to say, Lord, **I'm So Grateful**"*. Led by Gloria Griffin and Little Lucy Smith*

I, am so grateful - that I have Christ - in my life
What would my life be - without him
It would be very dark and drear

When I'm sad, he cheers me -
When I'm lonely - he will my comfort be
That's why I'm Grateful, truly grateful
That I have Christ, in my life . . . . . .

"Little" Lucy Smith & Gloria Griffin"
Photo: courtesy Eugene Smith collection

In the month of May, -Mrs. Roberta Martin Austin was the guest speaker at the Cathedral of Love Baptist

Church - 360 E. 75h Street in Chicago, serving as their Women's Day Speaker. Mrs. Martin was turning into quite a speaker. Later in that month, she and her singers sang at the Berean Bapt. Church, located at 5149 S. Dearborn for the Royal Club and The Associate Clubs of Berean at a program sponsored for Dr. & Mrs. C.D.L. Bradshaw. Mrs. Beatrice Winston Hall: Roberta Martin's sister served as co-chairman

Joe Bostic, one of the nation's leading African American radio personalities: heard on WLIB in New York City; sponsored the Festival of Gospel Music in New York City. At that festival, Joe brought together some of the nation's leading gospel personalities for a weekend of gospel enchantment. This July, The Roberta Martin Singers were one of the featured guests. This was one of the last services featuring the Roberta Martin Singers before they would go abroad.

In July, 1963; The Roberta Martin Singers were spotlighted at the Music Festival of Two Worlds in Spoleto, Italy. This was the first and only international trip for the group.

The
Roberta Martin Singers
board the airplane for Spoleto, Italy

Eugene Smith, Gloria Griffin, "Little" Lucy
Smith, Archie Dennis and Norsalus McKissick
Photo: courtesy Leonard Austin collection

Archie Dennis, Jr., Eugene Smith and Norsalus McKissick
During their trip to Spoleto, Italy

The billboard from the Festival of Two Worlds in Spoleto, Italy

ROBERTA MARTIN SINGERS

The Roberta Martin Singers in Spoleto Italy
(top: Archie Dennis, "Little" Lucy Smith, Norsalus McKissick
Bottom: Gloria Griffin & Eugene Smith)
doing what they do best: singing the gospel
photo: courtesy Leonard Austin collection

The Roberta Martin Singers in Spoleto, Italy
Photo courtesy: Chicago Public
Library - Lucy Collier collection

The Roberta Martin Singers in Spoleto, Italy
Photo courtesy: Chicago Public
Library - Lucy Collier collection

*** According to "Sonny" Austin; while overseas at the Spoleto Festival; part of their overseas journey included the Roberta Martin Singers singing for the British Royal family at Buckingham Palace in London England*

(August) - The Roberta Martin Singers were guest on the television program: Jubilee Showcase. This was their first public appearance since returning from Italy.

The Roberta Martin Singers

HOMECOMING PROGRAM
MON. Aug. 5th 1963 8pm
MT. PISGAH M.B. CHURCH
4600 S. PARKWAY
REV J. Wells, Pastor

Pictures of the Homecoming program
"Welcome Home from Overseas"

Eugene Smith, Archie Dennis, Gloria Griffin and Roberta Martin. Norsalus McKissick is leading.
Photo: courtesy of Leonard Austin collection

Archie Dennis, Gloria Griffin (leading), Eugene Smith, Norsalus McKissick; "Little" Lucy is at the piano, Joe Washington is on the organ and Delois Barrett Campbell. It looks as if Archie and Gloria are performing a duet. The gentleman behind Archie Dennis in glasses is Pastor Wells, pastor of Mt. Pisgah B.C. Mrs. Roberta Martin is sitting : facing Lucy.
Photo: courtesy of Leonard Austin collection

Also in **1963**, Chicago gospel music lovers and gospel music lovers across America paid their last respects to **Prof. Theodore Roosevelt Frye.** Frye, who was instrumental in giving Roberta Martin her musical start, and who was part of the Martin and Frye Quartet passed away after a brief stay in a local Chicago hospital. After a fitting tribute, his body was shipped to his homeland of Mississippi where he was laid to rest.

Mrs. Roberta Martin and Mrs. Sallie Martin
Photo: courtesy Leonard Austin collection

In late December, at the St. Luke Baptist Church on Chicago's Southside; the Roberta Martin Singers were once again featured singers at the home going of a beloved friend and colleague: this time it was the Blues great Dinah Washington. Dinah Washington: who was then Ruth Jones, sang as a young lady with The Roberta Martin Singers in the 1940's. Their fitting song that they sang in homage to the late Blues singer was a Dinah Washington favorite ***"The Angels Are Hovering Round"*** - of which Dinah (Ruth) led as a member of the group.

After the nation and the world mourned the loss of President John F. Kennedy in November, 1963; the New Year, **1964** brought a time of unified healing, renewed spirit and of unity and togetherness. It was also another exceptional year of musical, historical and cultural excellence for the Roberta Martin Singers.

(June) - Mrs. Roberta Martin Austin was honored by the Excelsior Club of the Mt. Pisgah Bapt. Church

Also on **June 3-4, 1964;** the Roberta Martin Singers once again ventured into the Savoy Studios to crank out some gospel masterpieces. At that session, the following personnel were in attendance:

Roberta Martin-piano; Little Lucy Smith-Organ; Delois Barrett Campbell-Soprano; Norsalus McKissick-Tenor, Eugene Smith-Baritone; Gloria Griffin-Alto; Archie Dennis-Baritone

Savoy Records, New York City
June 3, 1964
>He Merciful - Delois Barrett Campbell
>Didn't It Rain - Eugene Smith
>Keep The Faith - Norsalus McKissick
>Keep A Watchful Eye Over Me - Gloria Griffin
>Tell Jesus All - Little Lucy Smith
>*Singing The Gospel For The Lord - Unissued*

Savoy Records, New York City
June 4, 1964
>He Knows How Much We Can Bear - Roberta Martin
>Jesus Lifted Me - Roberta Martin
>Keep Me In Touch With Thee - Gloria Griffin & Lucy Smith
>The Failure Is Not In God, It's In Me - Norsalus McKissick
>When He Calls My Name - Archie Dennis

While once talking to Archie Dennis, he told me how the song, "When He Calls My Name " was conceived.

"We were traveling to a city to sing and I was sitting on the train and gazing out across the countryside. At that point a thought came to me. If God were to call me right now, no matter where I am, I will hear his name. I began to ponder the idea and I came up with the words- I don't know where I'll be, but I'll hear him when he calls my

name. I may be on the mountain-I don't know how far, or walking in the number that John saw".

That number and the others from that June 3-4, 1964 session became a part of the Savoy Album #14097 - "The Failure's Not In God, It's In Me".

"THE FAILURE'S NOT IN GOD; IT'S IN ME"
The Roberta Martin Singers - Savoy 14097
Recorded, 1964

Later in the month of **June 1964,** the Roberta Martin Singers were the special singing guest at the home going services for **Mother Lillian Brooks Coffey**: National Women's Director of the Church of God in Christ. This service was held at the Tabernacle Baptist Church in her hometown of Chicago.

(September) - Mrs. Roberta Martin Austin served as Mistress of Ceremonies for a program honoring Rev. Lucius Hall: noted radio personality.

(October) - Mrs. Roberta Martin Austin served as musical accompaniment for The Barrett Sisters at the Chicago Defenders 30th Home Service Show in Chicago.

Also in the same month, noted civil rights leader and national spokesperson, Ralph D. Abanathy was guest speaker at a program at the Mercy Seat Bapt. Church: located at 4015 W. Roosevelt. The Roberta Martin Singers served as special musical guest. After the service, Roberta

Martin and her husband, Jimmy Austin and several distinguished members of religious society in Chicago hosted a magnificent sit-down dinner for Rev. Abernathy at their home on Woodlawn Ave. Accompanying Ralph Abernathy was a young preacher who was climbing the national political ranks and was destined to be the next civil rights leader. His name was Martin Luther King, Jr.

(December) - Mrs. Roberta Martin Austin served as Mistress of Ceremonies at the Greater Harvest Baptist Church Yuletide program.

In February, **1965;** The Roberta Martin Singers were the guests at the anniversary of the Fellowship Baptist Church Choir of the Fellowship Baptist Church where Rev. Clay Evans was the pastor and LouDella Evans Reid served as Directress. Mrs. Roberta Martin Austin served as Mistress of Ceremonies

Also during the month of April, Roberta Martin Austin wrote and directed a gospel play, **"What God Hath Wrought"** spotlighting the evolution of gospel music. This was performed at the Mt. Pisgah Baptist Church: featuring a 200 voice choir with Madame Willie Mae Ford Smith as special guest. Staff included Prof. Willie Webb, Carolyn Saulsby & Eddie Wiliams. This play also showcased the literary writing talents of Mrs. Martin.

In the month of May, Mrs. Roberta Martin Austin served as Mistress of Ceremonies at the Birthday musical for Dr. Mollie Mae Gates: designer of Choir and Church Robes.

This event was held at the Allen Temple AME Church on 30th and Dearborn.

In June, Mrs. Roberta Martin and her singers once again took their yearly pilgrimage to the studios of Savoy Records. Accompanying Mrs. Martin were her cast of stars: Little Lucy Smith, Delois Barrett Campbell, Norsalus McKissick, Eugene Smith, Gloria Griffin and Archie Dennis. That session produced the following album:

"HE HAS DONE GREAT THINGS"
The Roberta Martin Singers - Savoy 14119
Recorded: 1965

He Has Done Great Things For Me - Gloria Griffin
I Know I've Got Religion - Norsalus McKissick
There IS A God - Delois Barrett Campbell
Standing On The Promises - Eugene Smith
Only What You Do For Christ - Archie Dennis
I'm Glad I'm A Witness - Gloria Griffin
The God I Serve - Norsalus McKissick
Teach Me How To Pray - Delois Barrett Campbell
Whisper A Prayer - Roberta Martin
Listen To The Lambs - Archie Dennis

September saw Mrs. Roberta Martin Austin headline the "Flower Musical": sponsored by the Gospel Choir of the Christ Temple Cathedral - 552 E. 44th

The fall of 1965 saw Mrs. Roberta Martin continuing her very busy schedule including: serving as Mistress of

Ceremonies at a program honoring Mde. Louise Overall Weaver at the New Covenant Bapt. Church and headlining the Women's Dept. at the Greater Progressive Miss. Bapt. Church - 1625-27 S. Lawndale in Chicago as keynote speaker.

As Eugene said,

"It was during this time that Roberta began to feel a little tired and complain about not feeling well. But that never stopped her from giving her all to those who helped to make the Roberta Martin Singers and the Martin Studio of Gospel Music thriving enterprises: God's precious children.

Mrs. Martin began **1966** by entering into the recording studios of Savoy Records: not with the Roberta Martin Singers, but with Delois Barrett Campbell, Billie Greenbey and Rhodessa Porter: **The Barrett Sisters.** On **February 11th, 1966;** Roberta Martin recorded the album, "Carry Me Back" with the Barret Sisters" with the selection, "Carry Me Back To Our Father's Praying Ground" serving as the signature tune. She is also serving as a background singer on all selections including: **I Hear God** of which Delois Barrett recently recorded with the Roberta Martin Singers on the album "It Was The Blood".

Also in February, Mrs. Roberta Martin & Prof. Alex Bradford headlined a program at the New Covenant Bapt. Church - 740 E. 77th in Chicago.

In March, 1966; Mrs. Roberta Martin Austin was the featured Women's Day speaker at Watley Temple: located on 4130 So. Indiana Ave.

Summer 1966 began for the Martin Singers with a trip once again back into the Savoy Studios. This time, Eugene Smith had recruited a new soprano singer in the person of Louise McCord of Detroit, Michigan. Louise McCord of Detroit, Michigan had previously sang with the Voices of Tabernacle before receiving the call from Eugene Smith. When Louise began singing with the Martin Singers, many times, Roberta was absent from the group: due to her illness. Not only did she cut her travels nationally; but also drastically cut her schedule of personal appearances locally. She did, however continue to write songs that bore that famous Roberta Martin touch.

When the Roberta Martin Singers went into the Savoy Studios on **June 16, 1966,** one of the songs recorded was possibly the last song, written by Roberta Martin. As one listens to the words of the song, you get the feeling that Roberta Martin had had a profound experience with God and was ready to meet her maker: and Louise was masterful at delivering the message musically. The song, "Just Jesus and Me" carries the lyrics:

> **Hand in hand, along the road we'll walk together**
> **Just Jesus and Me**
> **Heart to heart, we'll have a talk together**
> **Just Jesus and Me**

Closer than friends or brother
We're always, with each other
Everywhere I go, it's just Jesus
Jesus and Me . . . . . .

The personnel from the 1966 recording session were: Roberta Martin-contralto, Louise McCord-soprano, Gloria Griffin-alto, Archie Dennis-tenor, Eugene Smith-baritone, Little Lucy Smith-pianist and New Jersey's own Rev. W.J. Long on the organ.

"JUST ONE STEP AWAY"
The Roberta Martin Singers - Savoy 14147
* Ms. Louise McCord makes her debut on this album
Recorded: June, 1966

This I Believe - Gloria Griffin
Be Still, My Soul - Gloria Griffin & Lucy Smith
Wonderful IS He - Louise McCord
I Shall Be Like Him - Archie Dennis
He's The One - Eugene Smith
There'll Be Joy - Roberta Martin
Just Jesus and Me - Louise McCord
I'm Not Alone - Archie Dennis
One Step Away - Roberta Martin
My Lord and Master - Gloria Griffin

In August, The New Covenant Baptist Church Gospel Chorus presented "A Musical Tribute to Mrs. Roberta Martin". Later that month, Mrs. Roberta Martin Austin spearheaded a Birthday Celebration for Mrs. Joseph Johnson of Radio Station WVON.

In **1967,** the Roberta Martin Singers were continuing to sing and evangelize all over the country. Many times, when parishioners saw the Martin Singers, they did not see Roberta Martin. She had some years before, turned the groups management over to Eugene Smith and the musical arrangement to Little Lucy. Even though Roberta was not traveling with the group, the personnel of Little Lucy Smith, Eugene Smith, Gloria Griffin, Archie Dennis, Louise McCord and Norsalus McKissick were still carrying on the tradition of singing songs of zion on wings of love.

As Eugene once stated in a telephone interview concerning the latter years of Roberta Martin; he spoke the following: . . . . .

> *"Roberta Martin shared with me a dream that she had about a year and a half before her death. In this dream, she said that Jesus came to her and told her of a deeper walk with him that she was about to undertake. She said that he told her because of her faithfulness and dedication to him, that she ask whatever she wanted, and he would give it to her."*

In further talking to me, he shared with me that she (Roberta) told Jesus in this dream.

..."If I could have anything, I want to live with you forever and ever...All I want to do is to just wake up in glory".

In the month of May, Mrs. Roberta Martin Austin served as Mistress of Ceremonies for a benefit Organ Concert at the First Church of Deliverance - 4315 Wabash for Master Frederic Nelson III. In that same month, The Roberta Martin Singers were the special guest at the "Sermon In Song" program at the Progressive Community Church: located at 58 E. 48th Street honoring the Trustees Auxiliary for 45 years of service.

In December, **1967**; Mrs. Roberta Martin Austin served as the keynote speaker at the *Memorial Service Observance of Mrs. Magnolia Lewis Butts and Prof. Theodore Roosevelt Frye.* This program was sponsored by the Chicago Gospel Choral Union, Inc., at the Metropolitan Community Church. No one was more capable to present a moving and fitting tribute to the late Mrs. Butts and Prof. Frye than Mrs. Martin: who was musically mentored by the late Dr. Frye-back in the late 1920's and early 1930's at the Ebenezer Baptist Church.

The year of **1968** would test the faith of Mrs. Roberta Martin Austin as afflictions were a major part of her life during that time. As Eugene stated:

> *"Roberta was sick and made only limited appearances in and around the Chicago area. She did, however, receive a visit from an old friend, Mother Willie Mae Ford Smith. At that conversation, Roberta and Willie Mae talked*

about their journey to Heaven and how beautiful Heaven must be." She told her, "Willie Mae! If I die right now, it's just fine with me- for I'll be happy, in my home over there".

Although the long term effects of her illness had begun to affect the day to day mobility of Mrs. Roberta Martin Austin; she still managed to be a part of several church functions in and around the Chicago area.

In February, Mrs. Roberta Martin Austin appeared at the Apostolic Faith Church - 3818 So. Indiana Ave., for a program honoring Mrs. Della Mae Collins: Senior Choir Director.

In April, 1968; America and Black America in general mourned the loss of the great Dr. Martin Luther King, Jr. During this time, Eugene Smith and the Martin Singers rallied around the song, *"In These Dark Hours of Distress"* as a source of healing for the Nation for the fallen civil rights leader and as a source of personal consolation as we pray for our leader, Mrs. Roberta Martin. *"It was hard for us to go and sing and to know that our leader, Roberta was either at home and in and out of the hospital",* Eugene stated. He further orated that, *"But because of what she taught us, we carried on".*

Tho' sick and many times, exhausted; Mrs. Roberta Martin Austin continued to compose and arrange songs for her group, The Roberta Martin Singers. She also mustered enough strength and energy to venture back into the studios of Savoy Records along with the group for what would be her last recording session. The session, in mid **1968** featured an ailing Roberta Martin, Little Lucy Smith, Delois Barrett Campbell, Gloria Griffin, Archie Dennis and Eugene Smith. At that session, the Roberta Martin Singers recorded the following selections:

Praise God - led by Archie Dennis
I Have Hope - the last recorded song of Roberta Martin

"four songs from the old Apollo recording days"...
I've Got A Home For You - led by Archie Dennis
Come Into My Heart - once again led by Delois Barrett Campbell
After It's All Over - led by Archie Dennis
Saved – once again, led by Eugene Smith

Jesus Saviour, Pilot Me - led by Delois Barrett Campbell
He's Done Something For Me
Child of God - led by Little Lucy Smith and Delois Barrett Campbell
God's Amazing Grace

That recording session would truly be bitter sweet as it would be the last time the Roberta Martin Singers would record for Savoy Records and the last time that Roberta Martin Austin would ever record again. Savoy would release that album as "Praise God". When Roberta Martin sang "I Have Hope"; it was as if she was bidding the nation a fond farewell as she sung that song with vigor, strength, and spiritual upliftedness of knowing that her hope was only in Jesus.

"PRAISE GOD"
The Roberta Martin Singers - Savoy 14197
Recorded: 1968

*The last recorded album of the Roberta Martin Singers recorded, circa 1968. Mrs. Roberta Martin Austin passed away in January, 1969

Several selection on this album:
I've Got A Home For You, Come Into My Heart, Saved and After It's All Over were recorded on the old Apollo label in the 1950's.

changes:
originally I've Got A Home For You was recorded by Norsalus McKissick and carried a slower tempo. This version featured Archie Dennis, Jr. and carried a faster tempo. After It's All Over originally featured Roberta Martin and Eugene Smith as leads. On this album, Archie Dennis once again carries the lead on this selection.

In October, 1968; Mrs. Roberta Martin Austin observed what would be her last Women's Day Service at the Mt. Pisgah Baptist Church. She served as speaker and Mrs. Delois Barrett Campbell was guest soloist.

As the dawn of **1969** broke forth on the New Year's horizon; Mrs. Roberta Martin Austin was sweetly and tenderly just counting the moments away until her celestial departure. Having been sick and weak, she was not up to seeing company: including family and spiritual coworkers.

She was definitely not able to sing, play or compose music. It was as if she had finished her course, yet had kept the faith. And faith in God was all she had.

As with the words of the song, "Hand in hand; along the road we'll walk together: Just Jesus and Me"; Roberta Evelyn Winston Martin Austin walked home with God on Monday morning, **January 13, 1969**.

Although she was finally happy with Jesus alone, she had left an enormous following in her immediate family including husband James "Jimmy" Austin and son, Leonard "Sonny" Austin; her extended family of sisters, brothers, nieces, nephews; the singers of whom she nurtured: Roberta Martin Singers to her many church followers and friends. All were left behind to mourn her passing and celebrate her life. A gospel giant had ended her earthly reign and her heavenly journey had just begun. Although her songwriting and arranging had ended, her memories would live on for generations to come.

On a cold, wintry, January Chicago morning, in the year of our Lord, 1969; the family of Mrs. Roberta Martin Austin and the members of the famed Roberta Martin Singers laid to rest their immortal leader. As Eugene Smith stated, *"We had Roberta's funeral on Sunday evening and buried her the following morning. Lord it was as cold as I have ever seen it in Chicago and it snowed for days"*- but even through all of that, people from everywhere came to Chicago's Southside to the Mt. Pisgah Baptist Church to bid a fond farewell to Mrs. Roberta Evelyn Winston Martin

Austin: attesting to the fact that she was a true spiritual **"Moses"** in the field of gospel music.

Thomas A. Dorsey speaking at the funeral of Mrs. Roberta Martin
Photo courtesy: Chicago Public Library - Lucy Collier collection

Dr. Joseph Wells, pastor of the Mt. Pisgah Baptist Church and Roberta Martin's pastor officiated the services and singing great: Ms. Sallie Martin served as Mistress of Ceremonies. In addition to her husband, James "Jimmy" Austin, son Leonard "Sonny" Austin and immediate family members; an enormous number of business associates, personal friends and church acquaintances attended the homegoing celebration.

From **Mrs. Leona Price:** Mrs. Martin's personal secretary and manager of the Roberta Martin Studio of Music for many years; to **Dr. Theodore Charles Stone**-president of the National Association of Negro Musicians; from **Madame Mattie Moss Clark** – the national director of the music department of the Church of God in Christ; to the proclaimed father of gospel music: **Prof. Thomas A. Dorsey**; from **D. J. Robert Bradley** to gospel superstar **Clara Ward** – people came from all walks of life to pay respect to the lady who inspired so many to sing.

Finally and foremost; the members of the Roberta Martin Gospel Singers were all in attendance: celebrating the life of their spiritual leader. From the early day vocal talents of Robert Anderson, Norsalus McKissick, Willie Webb, Harold Lawrence (who came in the place of his brother James Lawrence) and Eugene Smith to the latter day reign of Roberta Martin pupils: Gloria Griffin, Archie Dennis, Jr., Romance Watson and "Little" Lucy Smith Collier (Mrs. Martin's step-dauighter).

From. Mrs. Delois Barrett Campbell, the group's first lyric soprano for many years: whose range combined the elements of a trained operatic singer coupled with the barrelhouse sound of a modern day "Ma" Rainey to Mrs. Bessie Folk: the first female member of the group whose rendition of *"Only A Look"* became the signature song of the Martin Singers. All paid homage to the late directress, singer, composer, pianist par excellence and arranger: not to mention businesswoman and church speaker.

After a soul inspiring service, Mrs. Roberta Martin was laid to rest at the Burr Oak Cemetery: along with other family members early on the next morning.

Order of Service

PROCESSIONAL
SELECTION —"Christ The Solid Rock" ..Mt. Pisgah's Combined Choirs
SCRIPTURE ....Reverend Goler
PRAYER ....Reverend Odell Young
SELECTION — "All My Hope" ....Mt. Pisgah Combined Choirs
    Soloist, Catherine Patrick
SOLO — "The Last Mile" ....Mrs. Gladys Beamon
TWO-MINUTE REMARKS —
    Mr. Thomas A. Dorsey
    Mr. Sid Ordower
    Mrs. A. C. Mitchell
    Mr. Theodore Charles Stone
SOLO — "How Great Thou Art" ....Mr. Archie Dennis
REMARKS —
    Reverend Sammy Lewis
    Reverend Cleophus Robinson
TRIBUTE TO ROBERT MARTIN AUSTIN ....Mrs. Leona Price
SOLO ....Mrs. Bessie Polk
REMARKS —
    Reverend E. R. Williams
    Reverend Eddie Williams
    Reverend William Vance
SOLO ....Mr. J. Robert Bradley, Nashville, Tennessee
RESOLUTIONS —
    Mt. Pisgah Social Club ....Mr. LaMar Creath
    Deacons and Trustees ....Deacon Eli Williams
    Gospel Choir ....Mr. James Markham
    Mt. Pisgah Church ....Mrs. Glendora Crenshaw Stokes
        — and —
    All Other Churches, Clubs and Organizations

ACKNOWLEDGEMENT OF
    CONDOLENCES AND TELEGRAMS ....Miss Annie Hurt
SOLO — "He Knows" ....Mrs. Delores Barrett Campbell
    and The Barrett Sisters
REMARKS —
    Mr. Kenneth Morris
    Reverend Frank W. Campbell
    Reverend F. D. Johnson
    Reverend J. C. Austin, Jr.
SOLO — "In My Home Over There" ....Robert Anderson
REMARKS —
    Reverend William A. Johnson
    Reverend Clay Evans
SOLO ....Miss Clara Ward, Los Angeles, California
REMARKS —
    Reverend Edmund Blair
    Reverend John E. Hopkins
    Reverend Maceo Woods
SOLO — "What A Friend" ....Miss Gloria Griffin
OBITUARY ....Mrs. Rosa Lee Lawson
SOLO — "Old Ship of Zion" ....Norsalus McKissick
EULOGY ....Reverend Joseph Wells
SOLO — "Good Night Beloved" ....Mr. Willie Webb

Roberta Martin's official program

Obsequies

Roberta Martin Austin

1912   1969

Sunday Evening, January Nineteenth
nineteen hundred and sixty-nine
at eight o'clock

MOUNT PISGAH BAPTIST CHURCH
4600 South Dr. Martin Luther King, Jr. Drive
Chicago, Illinois
Reverend Joseph Wells, Officiating
Mrs. Sallie Martin, Mistress of Ceremony

Roberta Martin's funeral program front cover

Honorary Pallbearers

Mr. Thomas A. Dorsey
Mr. Kenneth Morris
Mr. John E. Rodgers, Jr.
Mr. Calvin Williams
Mr. Sid Ordower
Mr. J. Robert Bradley

Active Pallbearers

Mr. Eugene Smith
Mr. Norsalus McKissick
Mr. Robert Anderson
Mr. Willie Webb
Mr. James Lawrence
Mr. Archie Dennis

— *Interment* —
Monday Morning, January Twentieth
From Mount Pisgah Baptist Church
To Burr Oak Cemetery at Eleven O'clock

Direction — Atkins Funeral Home

Roberta Martin's funeral program back cover

After the passing of Mrs. Roberta Martin Austin, the executives of Savoy Records paid a fitting tribute to the first lady of gospel music by creating a compilation of songs that she recorded with the Roberta Martin Singers during their tenure at Savoy Records. The album was entitled:

**"THE UNFORGETTABLE VOICE
OF ROBERTA MARTIN"**
A Memorial Tribute
*a compilation of selections Roberta Martin recorded
with The Roberta Martin Singers where she sang lead*

He Knows How Much We Can Bear
Sinner Man, Where You Gonna Run To
Ride On, King Jesus
Try Jesus, He Satisfies
When He Died
From Out Of Nowhere (live)
No Other Help I Know
I Shall Know Him w/Bessie Folk
One Step Away
Carry Me Back w/The Barrett Sisters

1912-1969
Photo: courtesy Leonard Austin collection

"Precious Memories"

- *All the photos in this section are courtesy of Leonard Austin*

Mrs. Anna Winston (Roberta's mother) center
Willie Webb – second from end on the left – next to him is Roberta Martin. Next to Mrs. Anna Winston: to her right is her son, Fontaine Winston: Roberta Martin's brother. Other members in the picture were unidentifiable

Little Sonny Austin – next to Sonny is Mr. William Winston – Roberta's daddy
back: James "Jimmy" Austin and Roberta Martin Austin

Roberta Martin, looking over requests that various church goers sent to her. She can't decide which one to sing.

Roberta Martin is on the far left. The lady on the far right is Clara Blanks: a very good friend of Roberta Martin's and her personal housekeeper. As Sonny fondly told the story, that in 1953, there was a fire at the 5430 So. Michigan Ave. residence and Clara and Roberta were going to throw Sonny out of the window in order to save him. He begged them not to throw him out of the window.

Louise Overall-Weaver, Ozella Weber, Roberta Martin, unidentified man, Novella Norton Tuck

(Brother & Sister) Fontaine Winston and Roberta Martin Austin: relaxing at the "Summer" cabin in Michigan

Roberta Martin with "Sonny" Austin on top of her favorite dog, "Reno". This was taken in the backyard on 5430 So. Michigan Ave.

Roberta Martin and her pet "Lobo" in Michigan

Jimmy Austin, Mrs. Roberta Martin Austin and unidentified lady enjoying an outdoor picnic

Zelma Winston- Mrs. Martin's cousin and personal hairstylist – who came to her house to do her hair every Saturday

Mrs. Martin listening to a composition being sung by an unknown singing ensemble. She is intently listening as to where she will place her musical expertise to create a polished Martin masterpiece. This photo was taken in the living room of the 4901 Woodlawn residence. The gentleman adjacent to Mrs. Martin is Donald Smith of the Maceo Woods Singers and the lady in front of him is a young Dorothy Norwood.

"Enjoying another Annual Day at Mt. Pisgah"
Mrs. Elizabeth Nightingale, Mrs. Ann Love,
Mrs. Roberta Martin, Mrs.; Mary Wells

The Roberta Martin Singers (1970 - 1981)

"Continuing the Musical Ministry without Roberta Martin"

With the passing of Mrs. Roberta Martin Austin in January of 1969; the singers continued for a short while- singing the gospel and continuing on in the Roberta Martin tradition: until totally disbanding the group and going into permanent semi-retirement in 1971. Several members of the group would, however, continue the tradition of singing the gospel: instilled into them by the late Roberta Martin.

Delois Barrett Campbell, the group's soprano singer for many years focused heavily on the success of her sisters group: The Barrett Sisters. She would, in years to come; travel all over the world: proclaiming the gospel in song with sisters Rhodessa Barrett Porter and Billie Barrett Greenbey and their musical accompaniments: including Charles Pikes: another protégé of Little Lucy Smith. She and her sisters would be a major part of a documentary about gospel music in 1982 called, "Say Amen, Somebody"

Gloria Griffin would move to California and produce a solo album with Little Lucy Smith accompanying her on several selections: revising the old Gloria-Lucy sound.

Archie Dennis, the group's tenor singer since 1959 would begin a successful career as a Praise and Worship leader for famed Evangelist Morris Cerullo. Archie would also, in later years, establish and pastor a successful church in the Pittsburgh area.

Louise McCord would continue to sing with the Voices of Tabernacle in Detroit, Michigan and produce a recording in 1969 with the Faith Temple Church of God in Christ

Radio Choir. She would later embark on a solo recording career.

In **1974,** some five years after her death, the Roberta Martin Singers came together again and were headliners at a gospel extravaganza in Detroit Michigan in which they sang in notable Martin Singers tradition.

Mrs. Leona Price, the manager of the Martin Studio of Gospel Music continued to manage the thriving music publishing house until her retirement in **1979.** Upon her retirement, James "Jimmy" Austin, the widow of Roberta Martin relocated and consolidated the business to 46th Street and King Drive.

Also in **1979,** Kenwood Records, a subsidiary of Nashboro Records in Nashville, Tennessee reissued: **The Roberta Martin Singers - The Old Ship of Zion**. This record was a compilation of some of the best selections that The Roberta Martin Singers produced during their heyday at Apollo Records: during the 1950's.

In the summer of **1980,** Dr. Bernice Johnson Reagon of the Smithsonian Institute in Washington, D.C., was commissioned to spearhead a project that would spotlight and highlight the music ministry of Roberta Martin. The objective was to describe an important era in gospel music and the place where Roberta Martin fit within that era.

In November, Dr. Bernice Reagon ventured to Chicago and met with six disciples of The Roberta Martin Singers: **Eugene Smith, Delois Barrett Campbell, Archie Dennis, Gloria**

Griffin and Bessie Folk. They were joined by **"Little" Lucy Smith** -who was once the pianist for the Roberta Martin Singers for a series of conversations and collectively they created a framework for rehearsals and a possible series of reunion concerts in the month of February, 1981.

At the suggestion of Dr. Pearl Williams-Jones, Dr. Bernice Reagon was accompanied to Chicago by noted gospel artist/pianist Richard Smallwood of Washington, D.C. Since a stroke in the early 1970's left "Little" Lucy with the inability to play the piano, the concert needed someone to play the piano who had a keen knowledge of the music and style of both Roberta Martin and Lucy Smith Collier. As a child, Richard Smallwood's early piano style of playing was patterned after Mrs. Roberta Martin and later, Little Lucy Smith. According to Eugene Smith, *"Richard was the perfect choice to serve as musical director"*. Rounding out the musical accompaniment was Charles Pikes, a true disciple of Little Lucy Smith; former musician of Mt. Pisgah Baptist Church and musical director for Delois Barrett Campbell & The Barrett Sisters.

After several intense rehearsals: involving singers *(Eugene Smith, Lucy Smith, Bessie Folk, Delois Barrett Campbell, Archie Dennis, Norsalus McKissick, Romance Watson, Gloria Griffin and Louise McCord),* the great Roberta Martin Singers were ready to once again carry the message of the Christ in song.

On **February 6, 1981**; 12 years after the passing of Mrs. Roberta Martin and 8 days before what would have been her 74th birthdate, The Roberta Martin Singers were once again assembled as a gospel singing group in the nation's capital of Washington, D.C., at the Smithsonian Institute of Natural History in the Baird Auditorium.

The official poster of the Reunion Concert
of the Roberta Martin Singers
February 6-8, 1981
Courtesy: Eugene Smith collection

At that series of events, the entire spotlight was on Roberta Martin and the music that she and her disciples: The Roberta Martin Singers produced.

At the educational seminars, along with Dr. Bernice Reagon were noted gospel historian **Dr. Horace Boyer:** a member of the Boyer Brothers gospel singing group, **Rev. Lawrence Roberts:** pastor of the First Baptist Church of Nutley, NJ and a recording executive who produced the Roberta Martin Singers during the Savoy recording days; and **Dr. Pearl Williams-Jones:** a leading scholar of African American music history and the daughter of the late Bishop Smallwood E. Williams- pastor of the Bibleway Holiness Church where the Roberta Martin Singers frequently visited yearly: from Palm Sunday to Easter Sunday. Each of these individuals painted a picture of Roberta Martin as an innovator of modern gospel music; a spiritual Moses and a virtual "Helen Hayes" of Gospel Music.

At the concerts held nightly, Dr. Bernice Reagon introduced the singers and set the tone for the nightly programs. Each night, Richard Smallwood and Charles Pikes provided musical accompaniment as the singers performed the music of Roberta Martin and in Roberta like fashion and style.

Friday Night, February 6, 1981
The Roberta Martin Singers in concert
Smithsonian Inst. -Baird Auditorium-Washington D. C.

The program began in the familiar Roberta Martin Singers fashion :

Only A Look - the theme of the RMS - led by Archie Dennis
The Lord's Prayer - led by Little Lucy Smith
I'm Not Alone - led by Archie Dennis

After the selection of *I'm Not Alone*, Eugene Smith came to the microphone and what he said, seemingly re-opened a chapter in gospel history. After over 12 years of nonexistent singing, Eugene Smith re-opened the program with the phrase, *"Once more and again, the Roberta Martin Singers"*. That phrase would serve as the foundational statement for the entire series of reunion services.

As Eugene set the tone for the next set of selections, the followers of the Roberta Martin Singers were treated to selections: many not having been heard or sung for over 30 years including:

Try Jesus, He Satisfies - led by Bessie Folk
Rock My Soul - led by Romance Watson
He's So Divine - led by Delois Barrett Campbell
I'm So Grateful - led by Gloria Griffin & Little Lucy
I Found Him - led by Norsalus McKissick

After the selection, ***I Found Him***, Eugene Smith began to tell each and everyone that the spectators came from all across America: including **Mr. Andrew Rowe:** who served as musician for the Roberta Martin Singers and traveled with them all across America during a time when Lucy Smith Collier was ill. He also began to name the family members of the Martin Singers who were in attendance and where they traveled from. After the acknowledgement of various special honored guest, Eugene then introduced the next selection, which featured Louise McCord.

Just Jesus and Me - led by Louise McCord

After the selection by Louise McCord, the piano began playing ***Precious Memories***. As they began to sing the selection, Archie Dennis gave the nightly benediction and the program faded into history as Norsalus McKissick continued to sing the selection: including the verse

"In sad hours, as I get lonely
The real truth of Jesus, love is told" . . . . . .
Jesus whispers, I'll be with you
What a comfort, to my soul. . . . . . .

Saturday Night, February 7, 1981
The Roberta Martin Singers in concert
Smithsonian Inst.- Baird Auditorium- Washington DC

The evening began with the Roberta Martin Singers (**Eugene Smith, Norsalus McKissick, Delois Barrett Campbell, Bessie Folk, Gloria Griffin, Little Lucy Smith, Archie Dennis, Romance Watson and Louise McCord**) taking their places on the platform. As pianist Richard Smallwood and organist Charles Pikes gave the musical introduction, the Martin Singers began in like fashion with the singing of *"Only A Look"* - theme song of the RMS - led by Archie Dennis - then followed by the Martin/Collier arrangement of *"The Lord's Prayer"* - led by Little Lucy Smith Collier.

Archie Dennis then struck out on *"What Would You Do Without Jesus"*. Eugene then began his masterful skill of narrating each and every song, starting with Delois Barrett Campbell singing *"There Is A God"*. After that, the Martin Singers gave a stirring rendition of one of their all time classics: *"Grace":* led once again by the skillful anointed voice of Norsalus McKissick. After a period of exuberant praising to God, the Roberta Martin Singers proceeded to expound on the next selection: **"Be Still, My Soul"**- led by the dynamic trio of Gloria Griffin, Archie Dennis and Little Lucy Smith. That song literally "tore up" the Martin Singers. Many of the singers were overcome with the spirit. As they regained their composure, Eugene reminded the audience that The Martin Singers did not perform concerts, "they had church service"; and they were truly living up to that slogan.

Eugene then called Delois Barrett Campbell to the microphone as she recreated the Little Lucy composition, *"He's So Divine"*. He then reminded us that…, **"there'll be a blessing, in store. For the meek and the poor, from the one whose so divine"**. As they were preparing to conclude the evening's services, Eugene told the audience on an incident a few days before the program. He said that he told Bessie Folk, as they were concluding the rehearsals that he should have mentioned the program to the Roberta Martin Memorial Club of the Mt. Pisgah Baptist Church. He then said, "oh well, can't worry about it now". Somehow the word got back to her and on that Saturday evening, Mrs. Dorothy White Spates, president of the Roberta Martin Memorial Club of Chicago was in attendance at Baird Auditorium. Eugene then had the members of the club to stand and receive a sentimental salute.

Bessie Folk then sang the song that Roberta Martin recorded back in the late 1950's, *"Sinner Man"*. Following that, Louise McCord continued with ***Walk On, By Faith***. As Louise put all that she had into that song, the auditorium once again, went up into sheer spiritual ecstasy. Romance Watson then crooned down memory lane with the singing on *"Talk About A Child That Do Love Jesus"*. "Old Man" Norsalus McKissick ended the program once again with the singing of *"Precious Memories"* as Rev. Archie Dennis gave the nightly benediction.

Sunday Afternoon, February 8, 1981
The Roberta Martin Singers in concert
Smithsonian Inst.- Baird Auditorium- Washington DC

Sunday afternoon, the final concert in the series of programs honoring Mrs. Roberta Martin and the Roberta Martin Singers would prove to be a historical event: both for the world of Gospel Music and for the Smithsonian Institute. This program would prove, in later years, to be "bittersweet" as it would be the last official program "service" where most of the alums of Roberta Martin would be present at the same time and in the same sanctuary.

As Dr. Bernice Reagon, coordinator for the series of programs for the Smithsonian Institute, introduced the members; Richard Smallwood, famed gospel pianist and Charles Pikes, pianist for the Barrett Sisters and both musicians inspired by the music mastery of "Little" Lucy Smith; Dr. Reagon called for The Roberta Martin Singers: **Eugene Smith, Norsalus McKissick, Gloria Griffin, Bessie Folk, Little Lucy Smith, Romance Watson, Archie Dennis, Louise McCord and Delois Barrett Campbell** to take their places. To thunderous applause, Archie Dennis once again opened the service with the familiar singing of the theme song, **"Only A Look"** followed by the Little Lucy Smith Collier arrangement of **"The Lord's Prayer"**.

As Richard Smallwood and Charles Pikes stepped up the pace on the musical instruments, Archie Dennis stepped up to the microphone and stirred the auditorium with the singing of **"Step In Jesus and Rescue Me":** the song that he first recorded with the Roberta Martin Singers on the Savoy album 14031- God Is Still On The Throne in 1959. Archie stated that ..."*All of those children, I know you fed; with two little fishes and five loaves of bread. Father up above, I know you rule the world .....Step in Jesus and rescue me"*

Eugene Smith then began to tell how the Roberta Martin Publishing House started. As Eugene spoke:

> *"Roberta would carry us from choir rehearsal to choir rehearsal those who would let us in – to introduce the music that today we call **GOSPEL**. Time went on and on and on – seems like a very slow pace. But we were just grateful. And one day, a young lady by the name of Phyllis Hall brought a song to Roberta Martin and from that day until now (1981), we have never looked back."*

As the musicians softly played in the background, Eugene began to proclaim those immortal words:

> *"We are our heavenly father's children and we all know that he loves us one and all – yet there are times – when we find an answer – to another's voice and call but if, we are willing – the Lord will teach us- his voice only to obey, no matter where- for he knows- Just, how much we can bear".*

At that point, Delois Barrett Campbell began to sing the song that in days past: Roberta Martin sang and literally tore up the country- **"He Know, Just How Much, We Can Bear."** After about ten minutes of spiritual excitement of "shouting and praising God"; Romance Watson took the spotlight with the singing of **"When He Sets Me Free".** Eugene then stepped back to the microphone and chanted those familiar words, **"won't you Try Jesus**, you tried everything else; won't you try Jesus, for he satisfies". Before he could get the words out, Bessie Folk was inviting the audience to "come unto Jesus, all ye that labor".

Although Bessie "slaughtered" the congregation with the singing of Try Jesus, He Satisfies; the onslaught of the Roberta Martin Singers was not over. Eugene then turned Norsalus McKissick loose on an already energized group with the singing of the classic, **"The Old Ship Of Zion".** When McKissick finished singing the classic, he then handed the mike to Gloria. When she finished singing **God Specializes**, in the midst of teary eyes; the audience in the hall of Baird Auditorium once again knew that the Roberta Martin Singers were still the legendary masters of Gospel Music.

As the service ended, the audience was reminded that immediately after this service, that the Roberta Martin Singers would once again grace the sanctuary of the Bibleway Holiness Church, located in Washington, DC, where Bishop Smallwood E. Williams was the pastor for a program entitled, *"An Evening with The Roberta Martin Singers".*

At that service, the Roberta Martin Singers truly let loose as they were truly at home: in the church setting. Much like a repeat performance of their "From Out Of Nowhere" album; the singers took the congregation from glory to glory to glory with such selections as *"Only A Look, Grace, God Is Still On The Throne, I'm Not Alone, The Old Ship of Zion and He's So Divine".*

The Roberta Martin Singers (1982 to present)

From Trailblazers to Living Legends and Beyond ......

After the series of historical services in Washington, DC. in February, 1981; the members of the Roberta Martin Singers soon returned to their various places of residence: Eugene Smith, Delois Barrett Campbell, Little Lucy Smith and Bessie Folk returned to Chicago; Norsalus McKissick and Romance Watson to Philadelphia; Archie Dennis to Pittsburgh; Louise McCord to Detroit; and Gloria Griffin to California to resume their day to day regimen. Of all of the members of the Roberta Martin Singers, Delois Barrett Campbell was the only singer who was still successfully touring and evangelizing the country with her group: The Barrett Sisters. Rev. Archie Dennis would soon organize a church in suburban Pittsburgh.

In **1982**; Mr. Jimmy Austin: the husband of the late Roberta Martin Austin and the father of "Little" Lucy Smith passed away. After the passing of Roberta Martin, Jimmy remarried Catherine Austin-a woman who sang with the Mt. Pisgah choir during the era of Roberta Martin. Leonard Austin, Mrs. Martin's son stated that:

> ***"I had no problems with Catherine marrying my father after mother had passed away. However, my real test came when I went back into our house on Woodlawn Avenue. I just knew that she had changed everything around. When I saw that she hadn't moved or touched anything that mother had placed there. I had a peace with the whole situation. She respected my mother's memory and took great care of my father".***

With the success of the Smithsonian reunion concert in February 1981, more successful concerts: several in the Philadelphia area; followed into the **1990's** featuring Eugene Smith, Norsalus McKissick, Gloria Griffin, Delois Barrett Campbell and Romance Watson. One such concert in **1993** also once again featured Richard Smallwood as their musical accompaniment- once again recreating the famed Roberta Martin sound.

With the **1990's** upon us and the new millennium of the year 2000 approaching, several members of the famed Roberta Martin Singers had reached their transitional time to depart from this earthly life to begin a life anew eternal.

First to make the earthly departure was **James Lawrence**: an original member of the Martin and Frye Quartet of 1933. He passed away in **1990**.

In **1994**, Southern Gospel music executives **Bill and Gloria Gather** brought together several black gospel music pioneers to Anderson, Indiana to produce a video featuring the music and the mastery of these noted black gospel artists. In attendance were several members of the Roberta Martin Singers: past and present. Robert Anderson sang, "He Knows Just How Much We Can Bear". Donald Vails led the congregation in "Only A Look" as a tribute to Mrs. Roberta Martin. Delois Barrett Campbell led "Let God Abide" and Eugene Smith narrated and set the stage as Gloria Griffin once again led "God Specializes": accompanied by Romance Watson, Eugene Smith, and Delois Barrett

Campbell. However, through several contractual legalities, the video wasn't released for sale; but excerpts from that historic session were later seen on social media.

A few years before Gloria Griffin and Norsalus McKissick passed away; the following members: Eugene, Norsalus, Romance and Gloria sang together in a concert in the city of Philadelphia for Johnny Lloyd and his Reunion Choir and for famed Philadelphia radio personality Linwood Heath.

In **1995,** three more members from the stable of Roberta Martin: **Gloria Griffin:** who recorded a succession of hits for the group including God Specializes, God Is Still On The Throne and I'm Grateful, **Myrtle Scott:** who recorded the classic, "I Know The Lord Will Make A Way-Yes He Will" and **Robert Anderson:** another original member of the Martin & Frye Quartet took their transitional flight to wake up in glory.

Norsalus McKissick: possibly the group's most successful lead singer who recorded such classics as Grace, The Old Ship of Zion, Precious Memories and God Is So Good To Me passed away on May 9, **1997** in Philadelphia.

In **1998**, the United States Postal Service, a branch of the Federal Government issued a postage stamp in honor of Mrs. Roberta Martin Austin, commemorating the achievements that she made to not only Gospel Music, but to American history. She was honored along with Mahalia Jackson, Rosetta Tharpe and the legendary Clara Ward.

On **May 4, 1999**; Professor **Willie J. Webb**; an original member of the Martin and Frye Quartet; organist for the Roberta Martin Singers prior to Little Lucy's tenure and founder of The Willie Webb Singers passed away

On **February 1, 2001**; **Bessie Folk**: the first female singer to join the Roberta Martin Singers in 1939 passed away. Later in that same year, **Rev. Archie Dennis, Jr.,** who had a succession of hits including: "Step In Jesus, When He Calls My Name and What Would You Do Without Jesus" passed away while successfully pastoring in suburban Pittsburgh..

Eugene Smith, a member of the group since 1934 and possibly Mrs. Martin's most trusted disciple and the manager of the group since 1949 passed away on **May 9, 2009**.

note: Eugene and Norsalus both passed away on the same day-12 years apart.

Mrs. Martin's step-daughter and the granddaughter of famed faith-healer: Elder Lucy Smith, **Little Lucy Smith Collier**, the group's musician for many years passed away on **September 19, 2010.**

Delois Barrett Campbell, the first lyric soprano of the Roberta Martin Singers: joining the group in 1943 and a member of The Barrett Sisters passed away on **August 2, 2011**

With the passing of Delois Barrett Campbell in 2011; the only surviving members of the Roberta Martin Singers are: Romance Watson of Philadelphia, Harold Johnson of Baltimore Md., and Louise McCord of Detroit, Michigan and Ann Yancey of Chicago, Ill..

Ever since the music ministry of Mrs. Roberta Martin and The Roberta Martin Singers began in 1933; there has never been a group of singers who exemplified gospel music more sincerely. Their singing and their styles of singing were often imitated but never duplicated. They broke new ground that had never been plowed and the results of their cultivating were extremely successful.

Roberta Martin created a piano style that had never been heard of or seen before. She took the barrelhouse style of such early day masters as Thomas Dorsey and Arizona Dranes to a new height when she added the element of a semi classical touch. Her in-service performances with her group on any selection would leave one in a spiritual trance.

Her publishing house brought forth a countless number of gospel classics: many still sung today in churches all across America and the message in those songs are still the same: Jesus Saves, Jesus Heals, Jesus Delivers. Many songwriters such as James Cleveland, Alex Bradford, Myrtle Jackson, Doris Ann Allen, Anna Shepherd and Jesse Dixon had her to thank for introducing their music to the gospel world: through the medium of sheet music with her publishing house being an outlet for national distribution.

Her singers, The Roberta Martin Singers, created a singing style that is still in existence to this day. The blending of male and female voices singing gospel music was an unheard of entity until Mrs. Roberta Martin received a vision from God and she chose to act upon that vision.

Her singers helped to mold the sound in the church choirs, groups and choruses. Many singers established their singing careers at the hand or aiding of Roberta Martin. Some of these singers were.....

Eugene Smith – whose narration style is still heard in the churches and gospel programs today

Little Lucy Smith – whose musical masterful touch has been emmulated by such greats as the late Charles Pikes: accompaniment for the Barrett Sisters and the great Richard Smallwood: founder of the Richard Smallwood Singers

Robert Anderson & Willie Webb – both founding members of the Martin & Frye Quartet who followed in Roberta's footsteps with gospel groups: both bearing their name. The Robert Anderson Singers, later the Good Shepherd Singers and later Robert Anderson and His Gospel Caravan would make a star out of Albertina Walker. Willie Webb, founder of the Willie Webb Singers would launch Alex Bradford to gospel stardom.

Delois Barrett Campbell – would later find international fame with her sisters: Rhodessa Porter and Billie GreenBey as the Famed Barrett Sisters of which Roberta Martin was their first unofficial musical accompanist.

Although Mrs. Roberta Martin Austin has been gone for over forty-five years, her memory lingers strongly in the hearts and minds of those she and her singers touched: from those visiting the publishing house to purchase sheet music to those singing in her church choirs at Ebenezer, Shiloh, South Park and Mt. Pisgah Baptist Church to the thousands touched by her singing in live services to the multiplied millions touched by her Fidelity, Apollo and Savoy recordings. Her greatest contribution was the development of a distinctive piano style and the integrating of male and female voices: of which she began in the late 1930's with Bessie Folk being the first innovator of the new "male-female" singing group.

During a time when there was no real standard in the group style of gospel singing; the Roberta Martin Singers of Chicago created a style that would ultimately be imitated; but never duplicated. Roberta Martin set a style for gospel singing and took nothing less than the perfected state of that style. She wrote and arranged music that touched the hearts and souls of those persons who heard her music and those who sang it.

Her singers were hand-chosen individuals who took each and every song to a new level of spiritual intimacy with the ending result always being a combination of the masterful message that the gospel song portrayed co-mingled with the artistic superiority that each vocal specialist displayed. The ending result was always the same: a sound that reached the heart, stirred the soul and purified the mind. Each singer's style of singing was uniquely different in that no two singers had a vocal quality that was similar. Likewise, the keyboard artistry of Roberta Martin, Little Lucy Smith and Willie Webb displayed three uniquely different yet closely-related styles that caused musical chords: when blended together; to create new unchartered areas of spiritual melodies and heavenly harmonies.

A great philosopher once said that a genius comes our way once every century. Thank you Roberta Martin for being that genius that came to us during the turn of the 20th century and for being the gospel mold, at a time when there was no mold. The lyrics of the last recording of Roberta Martin were very indicative of her life ***"I have hope, it's a beautiful hope; and it sets me free".***

In this new millennium and with the advent of social media; an entirely new generation of gospel music lovers are discovering or have discovered the music of Roberta Martin and her singers and the result is still the same: it gives strength to the weak; hope to the despondent and joy in a time of sorrow.

Now we come to the benediction of a legacy that has span for over eighty years of dedicated service. Most of the members of the Roberta Martin Singers have made their heavenly transition with only a few: Romance Watson, Harold Johnson, Louise McCord and Ann Yancey yet remaining with us.

As we come close to the end of this musical and cultural chapter in African-American history, let the words of this great Roberta Martin Singers tune serve as a lasting testimony to the memory of their greatness and to the lady who served as their spiritual Moses: Mrs. Roberta Martin.

"Keep a watchful eye, over me – lead me- from all danger, I plea
I feel, so all alone, though I'm tempted – make me strong
Let your presence, around me be... and keep a watchful eye, over me"

The Roberta Martin Singers

Recording Discography & Their Leader(s)
All selections prior to 1957 were released through Apollo Records, Fidelity Records or Religious Records of Detroit

Roberta Martin
    Didn't It Rain – 1947
    He Knows Just How Much We Can Bear – 1949
    What A Friend – 1950
    Where Can I Go – 1951 w/ Myrtle Scott
    You'll Understand It Better, Bye and Bye – 1951
    He Didn't Mind Dying - -1952 w/Myrtle Jackson
    After It's All Over – 1952 w/Eugene Smith
    I'm Gonna Praise His Name – 1953
    Do You Know Jesus – year unknown – w/Eugene Smith
    Sinner Man, Where You Gonna Run To – 1957
    Ride On, King Jesus – 1958
    He's Already Done, What He Said He Would Do – 1958
    That Great Judgment Day – 1959
    Try Jesus – 1960
    When He Died - 1960
    Cast Your Cares On Him – 1961
    No Other Help I Know – 1962 - w/Gloria Griffin
    I Shall Know Him – 1962 –w/Bessie Folk
    From Out of Nowhere – 1963 (live)
    He Knows How Much We Can Bear – 1964 (2nd recording version)

Jesus Lifted Me – 1964
Whisper A Prayer – 1965
One Step Away- 1966
There'll Be Joy – 1966
I Have Hope – 1968 *Her final recording

Eugene Smith

Jesus, Precious King – 1945 * other sources have it as 1949
He's All I Need – 1947
Nothing Can Change Me - 1947
Don't Wonder About Him – 1947
Pass Me Not, O Gentle Saviour – 1947 * unissued
I'll Follow In His Footsteps – 1949
Do You Know Him – 1950
Satisfied – 1950
I Am Sealed – 1951
Oh Lord, Stand By Me- 1952
Come In The Room – 1952
After It's All Over – 1952 w/Roberta Martin
I'm Too Close – 1952
Let God Abide – 1952
I'm Determined – 1952 w/Norsalus McKissick
Keep On Trusting – 1953
Is There Anybody Here – 1953
Marching To Zion – 1953
Shine Heavenly Light – 1954
He's Using Me – 1955
I'm Saved – 1955-
There's A Man – 1955

He's Always Right There – date unknown
Do You Know Jesus – date unknown
Walk In Jerusalem – 1957
Every Now and Then – 1957 w/Norsalus McKissick
The Crucifixion – 1957
In These Dark Hours of Distress – 1957
I Can Make It – 1958
That Great Judgment Day – 1959 w/Roberta Martin & Delois Barrett
He Laid His Hands On Me – 1959
Since He Lightened My Heavy Load – 1959
He Comes To See About Me – 1960
It's Gonna Rain - 1960
He's Leading Me – 1960
I Couldn't Hear Nobody Pray – 1961
All Things Are Possible – 1961
It Was The Blood – 1962
Look Up and Live – 1962 w/Bessie Folk
Come Lord Jesus- 1963
DIdn't It Rain – 1964
Standing On The Promises – 1965
He's The One – 1966
Saved – **2nd version** – 1968

Norsalus McKissick

Precious Memories – 1947
The Old Ship of Zion – 1949
My Eternal Home – 1950
He's My Light – 1952
The Old Account – 1952

Let God Abide – 1952
I'm Determined – 1952
Since I Met Jesus – 1953
I'm Just Waiting On The Lord – 1954
I've Got A Home For You – 1954
He's Using Me – 1955
Trouble In My Way – 1955
I Don't Mind – date unknown
Nothing But A God – 1957
Every Now and Then – 1957 w/Eugene Smith
God Is So Good To Me – 1957 w/Romance Watson
It's Amazing – 1957
Grace – 1958
I Found Him – 1958
He's All You Need – 1959
Hold Me Jesus In Thine Arms – 1959
If You Pray – 1960
I Need You Lord – 1960
Since I Met Him – 1961
Beyond The Dark Clouds – 1961
The Storm Is Passing Over – 1963
There Is No Failure In God – 1963
I Can Call Him Anytime – 1963
Keep The Faith – 1964
The Failure's Not In God; It's In Me – 1964
I Know I've Got Religion – 1965
The God I Serve – 1965

Bessie Folk
> Only A Look – 1945 * other sources have the recording at 1949
> Tell Jesus All – 1950
> I'll Do What You Want Me To Do - 1955
> Look Up and Live – 1962 w/Eugene Smith
> I Shall Know Him – 1962 w/Roberta Martin

Delois Barrett-Campbell
> Yield Not To Temptation – 1947
> My Friend – 1949
> What A Blessing In Jesus I've Found – 1949
> Let It Be – 1950
> Oh, Say So – 1953
> Come Into My Heart – 1955
> Only A Look – **2nd version** 1957
> Teach Me Lord To Wait – 1957
> He'll Make You Happy – 1958
> Back To The Fold – 1958
> He's So Divine – 1959
> Jesus Will Hear You Pray – 1959
> I Hear God - 1962
> The Best Things In Life Are Free – 1963
> He's Merciful – 1964
> There Is A God – 1965
> Teach Me How To Pray – 1965
> Come Into My Heart – **2nd version** – 1968
> Jesus Saviour, Pilot Me – 1968

Sadie Durrah-Nolan
There's Not A Friend Like Jesus – 1947

Myrtle Scott
Where Can I Go? – 1951 w/Roberta Martin
The Lord Will Make A Way, Yes He Will – 1951
I Wanna See Jesus – 1951

Myrtle Jackson
He Didn't Mind Dying – 1952 w/Roberta Martin

Romance Watson
When He Sets Me Free – 1957
God Is So Good To Me – 1957 w/Norsalus McKissick
Talk About A Child – 1958
Rock My Soul - 1958

Archie Dennis
Step In Jesus -1959
You've Been Truly Blessed – 1962
He Brought Me Out Of The Miry Clay – 1962 * issued as single
The Gateway To Life Is Christ – 1963
What Would You Do Without Jesus – 1963
When He Calls My Name – 1964
Only What You Do For Christ Will Last – 1965
Listen To The Lambs – 1965
I Shall Be Like Him – 1966
I'm Not Alone – 1966
Praise God – 1968

I've Got A Home For You – **2nd version** – 1968
After It's All Over – 2nd version - 1968

Gloria Griffin

Nobody Knows – 1957
Certainly Lord – 1958
God Specializes – 1958
God Is Still On The Throne – 1959
Hold The Light – w/Little Lucy Smith – 1959
Oh How Much He Cares For You – 1960
He Never Said A Word – 1960
Let's Go Home – 1960
Had It Not Been For Him – 1961
I'm His Child – 1961
I'll Keep On Holding, To His Hand – 1961
Walk On By Faith – 1962
Is It Nothing To You – 1962
No Other Help I Know - w/Roberta Martin – 1962
The Least That I Can Do – 1962
I'm Grateful – w/Little Lucy Smith – 1963
I Need The Lord – 1963
Keep A Watchful Eye Over Me – 1964
Keep Me In Touch With Thee – w/Little Lucy Smith – 1964
He Has Done Great Things For Me – 1965
I'm Glad I'm A Witness For My Lord – 1965
This I Do Believe – 1966
Be Still, My Soul – w/ Little Lucy Smith – 1966
My Lord & Master - 1966

Harold Johnson
Oh, What A Day - 1961

"Little" Lucy Smith
In These Dark Hours of Distress – w/Eugene Smith – 1957
Hold The Light – w/Gloria Griffin – 1959
Only God – 1961
I'm Grateful – w/Gloria Griffin – 1963
Tell Jesus All – 2nd version – 1964
Keep Me In Touch With Thee – w/Gloria Griffin – 1964
Child of God – w/Catherine Austin - 1968

Louise McCord
Wonderful Is He – 1966
Just Jesus and Me - 1966

The Roberta Martin Singers
& *The number 12*

After looking over a servies of events, it became ironic how well the number 12 and the career of the Roberta Martin Singers went hand in hand. Some events seemed co-incidental; while others seemed very strange . . . . .

1933 The Martin & Frye Quartet (Roberta Martin Singers) were formed in Chicago. **12 years later,** they made their first vanity recording in Hollowood California in 1945.

1935 Mrs. Ardie B. Smith Phillips was the first female singer to join the Martin and Frye Quattet. **12 years later,** in 1947; Mrs. Sadie Durrah; the 3rd official female singer to join the Roberta Martin Singers passed away and Mrs. Martin married Mr. Jimmy Austin.

1945 Rev. Rawls sponsored a program, The Battle Of Songs" which put Mahalia Jackson against Roberta Martin. This event was held at the Tabernacle Baptist Church in Chicago. **12 years later, in 1957;** the Roberta Martin Singers began recording for Savoy Records. **12 years after** that, Mrs. Roberta Martin Austin passed away in 1969.

Ironic, Norsalus McKissick and Eugene Smith passed award on the same date. May. 9. Norsalus died in 1997 and Eugene died in 2009: which was approximately **12 years apart.**

12 years after Mrs. Martin's death in 1969, the Smithsonian Institute in Washington, D.C., chose to honor her music in a three day educational symposium in 1981.

In 1938, Roberta Martin was singing "What A Friend We Have In Jesus" all over the East coast: touring with Bishop F.D. Washington and Mde. Ernestine Washington. **12 years later, in** 1950; she recorded that same selection for Apollo Records.

In **1956,** Roberta Martin began playing for the Mt. Pisgah Baptist Church. That merger would last for **12 years** as she resigned from the Mt. Pisgah Church in 1968.

In 1948, the Roberta Martin Singers were a huge success at the National Baptist Convention in Houston, Texas. **12 years later;** Mrs. Roberta Martin directed a 1000 voice choir on the selection GRACE at the National Baptist Convention in Chicago in 1960.

CPSIA information can be obtained at www.ICGtesting.com
Printed in the USA
BVOW08s1527050716

454464BV00001B/2/P